READING ETHNOGRAPHIC RESEARCH
A CRITICAL GUIDE

LONGMAN SOCIAL RESEARCH SERIES

Series Editor: Professor Maurice Craft, Goldsmiths' College,
University of London

Reading Ethnographic Research, 2nd edition
Martyn Hammersley

The Philosophy of Social Research, 3rd edition
John A. Hughes and Wesley W. Sharrock

The Limitations of Social Research, 4th edition
Marten Shipman

LONGMAN SOCIAL RESEARCH SERIES

Reading Ethnographic Research
A Critical Guide

Martyn Hammersley

2nd Edition

LONGMAN

London and New York

Addison Wesley Longman Limited
Edinburgh Gate
Harlow
Essex CM20 2JE
United Kingdom
and Associated Companies throughout the world

*Published in the United States of America
by Addison Wesley Longman, New York*

© Addison Wesley Longman Limited 1991, 1998

The right of Martyn Hammersley to be identified
as author of this work has been asserted by
him in accordance with the Copyright,
Designs and Patents Act 1988.

First published 1991
Second edition 1998

ISBN 0 582 31104 7

British Library Cataloguing-in-Publication Data
A catalogue record for this book is available from the British Library

Library of Congress Cataloging-in-Publication Data
Hammersley, Martin.
    Reading ethnographic research : a critical guide / Martyn
Hammersley. -- 2nd ed.
        p.   cm. -- (Longman social research series)
    Includes bibliographical references and index.
    ISBN 0-582-31104-7
    1. Communication in ethnology.   2. Ethnology--Authorship.
3. Ethnology--Study and teaching.   I. Title.   II. Series.
GN307.5.H35   1997
305.8'0072--dc21   97-29560
                                                                     CIP

Set in Times 10/12 by 43
Produced through Longman Malaysia, PP

CONTENTS

To Joan, Rachel, and Paul, again!

ACKNOWLEDGEMENTS

The work on which this book is based was carried out over a considerable period of time, and I am grateful to many colleagues for their assistance, including Stephen Ball, Jeff Evans, Andy Hargreaves, John Scarth, Thomas Schwandt, John K. Smith, and Peter Woods. Barry Cooper, Peter Foster, Roger Gomm and Donald Mackinnon must be singled out for particular thanks for responding to some of my recent work with detailed comments. They are the closest approximation I know to the model of the research community outlined in Chapter 3. They have shaped this book in many ways, not least in those respects in which (to varying degrees) they remain sceptical! Finally, once again, I thank my family for their forbearance.

PREFACE

There is now a considerable literature dealing with ethnographic or qualitative methodology, including many texts for students. However, this literature concentrates very largely on how to *do* ethnographic research. Very little attention has been given to how we should *read and assess* the studies it produces. Yet this is a crucial task, and by no means straightforward.

We tend to treat reading as a skill that is learned when we are children, as if it were something that had a well-defined end. But, in an important sense, we are always (or should always be) still learning how to read. A little reflection reveals that reading implies understanding, and that the process of understanding texts is a complex matter that is closely bound up with the nature of the ideas that writers seek to communicate, and with our own background knowledge and experience. Most obviously, there are texts whose vocabulary we may not comprehend, for example those that rely on esoteric mathematical symbols or that are written in unfamiliar natural languages. But even when we understand the grammar and vocabulary employed, we may not always understand the message intended. A mundane example of such lack of understanding happened to me when visiting friends. The son of the house (who was cooking the evening meal) said: 'Tell my mother she looks like a vegetable'. I understood the meaning of the words, but I could not understand the purpose (and therefore the meaning) of the message. It only made sense when I discovered later that his mother had told him that if he cooked her any more vegetarian meals she would look like a vegetable! Understanding is not given merely by knowledge of the meanings of the words used, then, it also depends on the context in which communication occurs and the motivation for the message built into that context. Similarly, in seeking to understand a written .text, we must ask: what issues are being addressed, in response to what earlier contributions, and why (Tully 1988) Furthermore, the context of a communication is almost endlessly extendable. Understanding it may involve taking account of the wider society in which it occurs and even of the history of that society. And, usually we are concerned not just to understand, but also to learn and to use. At one level this may be a matter of deriving information from what we read, and implicit in this is assessment of the validity and value of that information. Equally, though, what we read may stimulate lines of thinking that owe much more to our own concerns and knowledge than to the message of the text.

The complexity and importance of reading has long been recognised in the humanities. From at least the time of the Renaissance there has been a concern with how to understand texts produced in earlier periods, especially the writings of the Ancient Greeks and Romans, and of course the Bible. The Humanists were aware of the cultural differences between the societies from which these texts came and their own, and the problems of understanding that this could cause. In the Anglo-American world much of this interest in understanding texts has come to be concentrated in the discipline of literary studies. Early in the twentieth century the influence of what was labelled the 'new criticism', especially the work of I.A. Richards, placed great emphasis on reading. One of Richards' books is entitled *How to Read a Page* (Richards 1943). Of course, there have been many changes in literary studies since the time of Richards, but if anything there is now even greater emphasis on the active, critical and creative character of reading.[1]

Reading is not a simple matter, then. And in the case of ethnographic research reports this is an especially important point. The style in which these are written is to a large extent non-technical: it is modelled on forms of expression that we are familiar with in everyday life, such as those found in travel writing, newspaper articles and even novels. It may be concluded from this that such reports are straightforwardly readable by anyone. Indeed, ethnographers sometimes claim this to be one of the great virtues of their accounts, in comparison with reports based on quantitative analysis. This is deceptive, however. In some ways the familiar character of ethnographic writing makes it more difficult to read and assess properly. A colleague of mine once formulated a tentative law about the ethnographer's task of gaining access to settings in order to study them. Atkinson's hypothesis states that the easier it is to gain access, the more troublesome life in the field will be for the ethnographer (Atkinson 1981b). It seems to me that something analogous may apply to research texts: the more immediately accessible they seem, the more difficult they may be to read properly and assess. This is intended as no more than a warning: apparently easily understandable texts can turn out to have meanings that are less straightforward than initially appears.

The form that reading should take depends in part on our purposes. When reading for entertainment we are likely to adopt a different approach from when we study a text in order to understand it in some deeper sense. Furthermore, we may adopt different approaches depending on the character or detail of understanding we require. My concern in this book is with reading ethnographic studies for the purpose of coming to reasonable judgements about the value that the claims they make have in research terms. This is the sort of reading and assessment that is (or ought to be) characteristic of the way researchers review one another's work, in private and public, as well as that appropriate for students working on literature relevant to their courses and projects. There are other ways of approaching ethnographic texts, however: in terms of identifying and describing the linguistic and rhetorical resources they employ, how they came to be written, what they signify about the context that produced them, and so on. Such matters may be of relevance to the kind of reading I am concerned with here, but only as background. Equally, ethnographic research may be assessed for how well it helps to solve practical problems, or for what it can tell us about the competence of the researcher and/or about the effectiveness or ethical status of the research strategies employed. While I touch on some of these issues, they are not the main concern in this book.

Reading plays an important (and rather neglected) role in science and scholarship. These are collective enterprises and the work of any individual researcher needs to be coordinated with that of others. More than this, though, the intellectual authority of scholarship and science depends on the communal assessment of its products. It is largely because scientific claims are (or are assumed to be) subjected to systematic and rigorous assessment by fellow scientists that we tend to treat them as more reliable than the views of non-scientists; though, of course, our confidence is not always justified. Even in the case of the natural sciences, this process of monitoring and communal assessment cannot *guarantee* the validity of the results. But, for a variety of reasons, the process is somewhat less effective in the social sciences (including ethnography). One of my hopes is that this book may encourage more, and more effective, assessment of ethnographic studies. It has often struck me that the amount of time and care spent producing ethnographic accounts is probably not balanced by sufficient attention to the understanding and assessment of those accounts on the part of readers. Certainly, the space given in journals and books to the presentation of the findings of new research is very much greater than that devoted to the detailed assessment of such work by others.[2]

For students on social science courses, the reading of 'ethnographic and other kinds of studies is essential and inescapable. But, as I noted earlier, very often little guidance is given about how to do this. It is the purpose of this book to provide such guidance, based on my own experience both of doing ethnographic research and of reading it. I am convinced that we can learn from one another's experience, in this area as in others. That said, I must emphasise the limits of what can be offered by this book. First, it is not based on a consensus among ethnographers about how to approach reading their work. As we shall see, there is considerable disagreement about the nature of ethnography, and about the standards by which it should be assessed. Second, what is presented here is not a set of steps which, if followed, will guarantee 'good reading'. No formulae of this kind are available. Third, what I have to say is limited to only one part of the process of understanding: the identification and assessment of the claims and conclusions presented by the author. I do not deal with the more creative and reflective levels of reading, but the latter may be more fruitful if based on sound understanding and assessment of the more mundane kind that I am concerned with here.[3]

What I provide in this book, then, is a framework of ideas for thinking about and approaching the reading and assessment of ethnographic texts. It is not offered as the only way that this can be done, though it is the best that I can suggest at the moment. Many ethnographers will not like one or other aspect of what I recommend (and some may not like any of it!). So, as reader of this text, you may well question what I have written here. That is all to the good. I hope that your reading of this book will be as reflective and critical as the sort of reading of ethnographic texts that I advocate in it.

Outline of the book

This second edition follows much the same plan as the first. I have taken the opportunity to correct errors (though no doubt also to introduce one or two more!), to clarify the discussion where necessary, and to change some of the examples. The only major difference concerns value claims. In the first edition these were treated as a legitimate part of ethnographic accounts. I no longer believe this to be true, and so in this new edition I have tried to draw a clear distinction between evaluations, on the one hand, and descriptions and explanations, including those that rely on a value framework, on the other. However, I have retained a brief discussion of what is involved in the assessment of value claims, because when such claims *are* made it may be necessary for them to be considered.

The first chapter provides a sketch of ethnography and of recent developments in methodological thinking about it. I emphasise the diverse nature of the ethnographic tradition, and look at some of the key debates about the scientific status of the work it has produced. Chapter 2 is concerned with the process of understanding ethnographic texts in the narrow sense of identifying what the author was seeking to communicate, and why. Clearly, such understanding is an essential preliminary to any assessment of the claims and conclusions of a study. An overview of what is involved in assessing ethnographic texts is provided in Chapter 3. Of special importance here is the question of the standards by which they should be judged. This question raises some fundamental issues about the nature of ethnographic research. The next two chapters, 4 and 5, discuss what I take to be the two main assessment standards that should be applied to ethnographic studies: validity and relevance. In Chapter 6 I illustrate the approach to understanding and assessment that I have advocated by applying it to an example of my own work. Finally, Chapter 7 widens the focus, locating the sort of assessment with which I have been concerned in a broader context that takes in other kinds of assessment.

Notes

1. Richards' book followed closely on the heels of Adler's *How to Read a Book* (Adler and van Doren 1972). Spivak's 'How to read a "culturally different" book' continues the series in a way that illustrates how conceptions of understanding a text have changed (Spivak 1994). For accounts of more recent approaches to literary studies, see Norris (1982), Eagleton (1983) and Newton (1990).

2. There is, of course, much reviewing of ethnographic books but often the reviews are brief and superficial. The following are examples of more extended assessments of particular ethnographic studies: Blumer (1939), D.H. Hargreaves (1978), Freeman (1983), West (1984), Hammersley (1990a and b), Foster (1990), Foster *et al.* (1996).

3. There are a few other books dealing with understanding ethnographic texts. Jacobson (1991) and Atkinson (1992) pay particular attention to the various ways in which ethnographic texts structure their arguments; the former carries out assessments of key examples from the anthropological literature. There are also some books that deal with the assessment of social research in general: for example, Tripodi *et al.* (1969), Katzer *et al.* (1978), Stern (1979), Rose (1982), Light and Pillemer (1984), and Black (1993).

CHAPTER 1

The nature of ethnography

The term 'ethnography' is not clearly defined in common usage, and there is often disagreement about what count and do not count as examples of it. Furthermore, the meaning of the term overlaps with that of several others – such as 'qualitative method', 'interpretative research', 'case study', 'participant observation', 'life history method', and so on. Nor are *these* terms used in very precisely defined ways.[1] In part, this diversity and looseness of terminology reflects some disagreement, even on fundamental issues, among advocates of these approaches. It also results, perhaps, from a certain vagueness in thinking about methodological matters that arises from widespread emphasis among ethnographers on the primacy of research practice over 'theory' about how to do it. Sometimes this amounts to an anti-theoretical or anti-methodological prejudice. Ethnographers often tend to distrust general formulations, whether about human social life or about how to do research, in favour of a concern with particulars. In some ways, this is healthy: methodology cannot tell us what to do, it can only provide guidelines and cautions. But, however much one distrusts methodology, one cannot escape it. As we shall see, the practice of ethnography is surrounded by a host of methodological and philosophical ideas. And, while we must recognise the limits of abstract reasoning, we should press it as far as it will go in providing illumination, whether as regards doing research or reading and assessing its products.

I will examine some of the philosophical ideas associated with ethnography later in this chapter. First, though, I want to look briefly at the forms of research design, data collection and analysis that are characteristic of it, and to sketch something of its history.

Ethnography as method

In terms of method, generally speaking, ethnographic research has most of the following features:

1. People's behaviour is studied in everyday contexts, rather than under conditions created by the researcher, such as in experiments.
2. Data are gathered from a range of sources, but observation and/or relatively informal conversations are usually the main ones.
3. The approach to data collection is 'unstructured', in the sense that it does not involve following through a detailed plan set up at the beginning, nor are the categories used for interpreting what people say and do entirely pre-given or fixed. This does not mean that the research is unsystematic; simply that initially the data are collected in as raw a form, and on as wide a front, as is feasible.
4. The focus is usually a small number of cases, perhaps a single setting or group of people, of relatively small scale. Indeed, in life history research the focus may even be a single individual.
5. The analysis of the data involves interpretation of the meanings and functions of human actions and mainly takes the form of verbal descriptions and explanations, with quantification and statistical analysis playing a subordinate role at most.

As a set of methods, ethnography is not far removed from the sort of approach that we all use in everyday life to make sense of our surroundings. It is less specialised and technical in character than approaches like the experiment or the social survey; though all social research methods have their historical origins in the ways in which human beings have always gained information about their world. The more specific origins of ethnography lie in the writings of travellers concerned to inform their fellows about other societies, whether it is Herodotus exploring the western provinces of the Persian Empire (Rowe 1965) or Hans Stade reporting on his captivity by the 'wild tribes of Eastern Brazil' (Pratt 1986). These other societies were not always geographically distant either. Thus, in the nineteenth century, we have Friedrich Engels, the son of a German industrialist, investigating the lives of Lancashire factory workers, Tocqueville reporting on *Democracy in America*, and Henry Mayhew writing newspaper articles about working class life in London (Engels 1892, Tocqueville 1966, Mayhew 1861–2 and 1971).

The writings of such people form the early history of the disciplines now called social or cultural anthropology and sociology.[2] However, the data on which these reports were based were often unsystematic and sometimes misleading; and the analysis was frequently speculative and evaluative (though sometimes valuable for all that). One of the most important features of the development of social science disciplines in the nineteenth and early twentieth centuries, under the influence of the model of the natural sciences, was the attempt to overcome the methodological deficiencies of earlier accounts. In the nineteenth century anthropologists tended to rely on the reports of travellers and missionaries for their data, but from around the turn of the twentieth century it became widely accepted that it was necessary for them to collect their own data, and to do so in a systematic and rigorous manner. Initially, this tended to take the form of expeditions that were primarily concerned with collecting artifacts, both material and non-material (such as myths). Later, particularly through the influence of Bronislaw Malinowski, it came to be required that the anthropologist live among the people being studied, learn their language, and observe their lives firsthand.[3] In addition, anthropologists became much more concerned with avoiding the speculative excesses of their predecessors, and with adopting a scientific approach to the interpretation of evidence. Since the early decades of the century, ethnography has been the staple research method employed by social and cultural anthropologists, though they have sometimes combined it with social survey work and even with the use of psychological tests.

Sociologists have also employed ethnographic methods since early in the twentieth century, though it has not occupied as central a place in their discipline as it has in anthropology. One of the earliest developments here arose in what is sometimes referred to as the 'Chicago School of Sociology'. Chicago was among the first universities in the United States to establish a sociology department, and that department was very influential in the 1920s and 1930s. Sociologists working there became preoccupied with the character of their city. It had experienced a tremendous growth in size in the 20 years each side of the turn of the century, and many of the new inhabitants were European immigrants. Given this, Chicago sociologists came to see the city as a kind of natural laboratory in which the diversity and change characteristic of human behaviour (and particularly of modern social life) could be studied. While investigation of the city had begun before his arrival, Robert Park, an ex-newspaper reporter, was the main force behind the series of studies produced by students at Chicago in the 1920s, 1930s and 1940s. Some of the work carried out was statistical in character, but much of it took the form of what was called 'case study research'. This involved detailed investigation of a single case, or a small number of cases, these being areas of the city (as with Zorbaugh's 1929 exploration of the different parts of North Side Chicago and their inhabitants), city organisations (for example, Cressey's 1932 study of the taxi-dance halls where men paid the dancers a fare for each dance), or even individual people (as in the case of Shaw's 1930 *The Jack Roller*, a life history of what we would now refer to as a 'mugger'). These studies used methods that approximated the ethnography of today, though they tended to place greater emphasis on written documents.[4]

At around the same time as the Chicagoans were engaged in studying their city, another important source of ethnographic method in sociology and anthropology was emerging: what came to be called the 'community study'. The inspiration for this was in large part the application of anthropological methods to the study of Western societies. One of the first and most important community studies was the investigation of 'Middletown' (the small town of Muncie, Indiana) by Robert and Helen Lynd. On the basis of participation and observation in the community and interviews with community members, they described key aspects of life in Middletown: 'getting a living', 'making a home', 'training the young', 'using leisure', 'engaging in religious practices', and 'engaging in community activities'. This specification of aspects of community life derived from a scheme developed by anthropologists for studying non-Western societies. The Lynds had originally been concerned with religious beliefs and practices, but they realised that these could only be understood in the context of community life as a whole (Lynd and Lynd 1929). Following this, many other communities, usually but not always small towns, were studied; and sometimes they were restudied. The Lynds themselves returned to Middletown some ten years after their first investigation, to document the changes that had occurred, and especially the effects of the Depression (Lynd and Lynd 1937). Later, a similar tradition of studying small communities was established in Britain, producing, for example, Williams' book about the village of Gosforth (Williams 1956), Emmett's account of Llanfrothen (Emmett 1964), and Stacey's study and restudy of Banbury (Stacey 1960, Stacey *et al.* 1975). In addition, a number of investigations were mounted by the Institute for Community Study in the 1950s and 1960s, most notably of working-class areas in London (see Platt 1971). This community study tradition has witnessed a decline in the past 20 years, in both the United States and Britain; though there have been some recent studies of aspects of community life in the West by anthropologists (see, for example, Cohen 1982 and 1986).[5]

As I noted, a crucial element of the emergence of specialised social sciences was the drive to make them systematic and rigorous, on the model of natural science. However, this took a variety of forms, depending on what were believed to be the essential features of science, and ideas about the extent to which and ways in which human social life differed from the subject matter of the physical sciences. As we saw, within anthropology, it resulted in an emphasis on more direct observation by the anthropologist and attempts to make the descriptions produced as objective as possible, being neither deceived by the historical myths of the natives nor blinded by one's own cultural assumptions and prejudices. An analogous emphasis on documented and first-hand information was the initial effect of the drive for scientific status in sociology, as represented by the early Chicago School. However, from at least the 1930s onward, at Chicago and elsewhere in the United States, social science came increasingly to be associated with the statistical method; and by the 1940s and 1950s survey research was the dominant method within US sociology. This is not to suggest that case study and community study work ceased. Research in anthropology continued much as before. Even in sociology, ethnographic studies still appeared, notably William Foote Whyte's (1993) *Street Corner Society* (an investigation of the cultures to be found among young males in an Italian American community) first published in 1943, and the work of Everett Hughes and his students on various occupations and on medical and educational institutions. In addition, partly stemming from the dominance of quantitative method, there were increasing efforts to enhance the rigour of ethnographic research.[6]

However, in the 1960s the overwhelming dominance of survey methodology in US sociology and elsewhere started to wane, and ethnographic research became more widely advocated and practised (though survey research has remained very influential in the United States, more so than in Britain). The growth in ethnography at this time was especially notable in the study of deviant groups, but also in the sociology of medicine and other areas. In Britain there was a relatively sudden increase of interest in ethnographic research towards the end of the 1960s, largely as a result of the diversification of theoretical approaches to include symbolic interactionism, phenomenology and ethnomethodology. A considerable body of British ethnographic research has been produced since then, especially in the sociologies of deviance, medicine and education.[7] And this resurgence of interest in ethnography in the 1960s, 1970s and 1980s, following a period in which survey research had become almost identified with sociological method, was accompanied by considerable debate about methodological issues. This occurred not just between advocates of survey and ethnographic research, but also among ethnographers themselves. In the next section I want to look briefly at these discussions.

Methodological debates about ethnography

Debates about ethnography can be broadly divided into two categories, with the first preoccupying discussions in the 1960s and 1970s, the second becoming more salient in the 1980s and 1990s:

1. Those centring on criticisms of ethnography for not meeting the criteria assumed to be characteristic of science.
2. Those concerned with arguments that ethnography has not broken sharply enough with, or moved far enough away from, quantitative research and the model of natural science.

I will look at each of these two sorts of debate in turn.

Criticism of ethnography for not being scientific

Within sociology, competition with quantitative approaches, and especially with survey research, has long shaped the way in which ethnographers have thought about their work, raising the question: is ethnography scientific? By the 1960s, quantitative research in the form of experimentalism and social surveys had become highly developed, and sophisticated methodological literatures had grown up around them which took it for granted that they were implementing scientific method. While there was dissensus about some points, there was considerable agreement on the basics, and in large part this was framed in terms of the positivist outlook that had dominated the philosophy of science in the 1940s and early 1950s. Central here was the idea that what was required in empirical research was clear and operational specification of hypotheses; the selection of a research design that allowed those hypotheses to be tested, either by the physical manipulation of variables (as in experiments) or through statistical analysis of large samples of cases (as in survey research); along with the assessment of measurement error by means of reliability (and, more rarely, validity) tests.

Ethnographers responded in several ways to this influential view of the nature of social science methodology:

1. Some claimed that ethnography is *more* scientific (that is, closer in character to natural science) than quantitative research. In the early decades of the twentieth century, this was argued on the grounds that case study can produce universal laws, not just the probabilistic findings characteristic of statistical method (Znaniecki 1934). This argument is rarely used today, both because of the statistical character of some parts of more recent work in physics (notably quantum theory), and because most ethnographers have lost faith in the possibility of discovering sociological laws. Later, it was more common to find the scientific character of ethnography being justified on the grounds that it is more suited than are experimental and survey research to the nature of human behaviour, in particular its processual and meaning-laden character (Bruyn 1966, Blumer 1969, Harré and Secord 1973).

2. A second sort of response involved broadly accepting the view of sociological method characteristic of quantitative research, but treating ethnography as distinctive in its suitability to particular phases of the research process or to particular research problems. For example, it was often regarded as useful in the pilot stages of social surveys, or in the debriefing phases of experiments; and/or it might be seen as well-suited to the study of particular types of people, for example deviant groups, whose small numbers and/or inaccessibility make them difficult to survey. On this view, ethnography could be usefully combined with other methods, which are assumed to have complementary strengths and weaknesses.[8]

3. A third position was that ethnography represents a different kind of science to that characteristic of the natural sciences, and quantitative method was criticised for aping those sciences. Often associated with this view was the claim that ethnography is idiographic rather than nomothetic (that it focuses on the unique as much as the general), and/or interpretative rather than observational (that the understanding of human behaviour always involves interpretation, not mere physical description).[9]

In their methodological writings ethnographers frequently combined these three positions in various ways, and not always with great consistency. The first and third were typically given the most emphasis, with ethnography viewed as based on distinctive assumptions about human society, and about how it could be best understood, that diverge from those implicit in most quantitative research.

The assumptions seen as distinctive to ethnography can be summarised under the headings of naturalism, understanding and discovery:

1. *Naturalism.* This is the view that the aim of social research is to capture the character of naturally occurring human behaviour, and that this can only be achieved by first-hand contact with it, not by inferences from what people do in artificial settings (such as experiments) or from what they say in interviews about what they do in *other* settings. This is the reason that ethnographers carry out their research in 'natural' settings, settings that exist independently of the research process, rather than in those set up specifically for the purposes of research. Another important implication of naturalism is that in studying natural settings researchers should seek to minimise their effects on the behaviour of the people being studied. The aim of this is to increase the chances that what is discovered in the setting will be generalisable to other similar settings that have not been researched. Finally, the notion of naturalism implies that social events and processes must be explained in terms of their relationship to the contexts in which they occur. What is involved here is an appeal to what is sometimes called the 'pattern model of explanation' as against the covering law model characteristic of positivist philosophy of science.[10]

2. *Understanding.* Central here is the argument that human action differs from the behaviour of physical objects, and even from that of other animals: it does not consist simply of fixed responses or even of learned responses to stimuli, but involves *interpretation* of stimuli and the *construction* of responses. On occasion, this argument reflects a complete rejection of the concept of causality as inapplicable to the social world, and an insistence on the freely constructed character of human actions and institutions. Sometimes, however, it is claimed that causal relations *are* to be found in the social world, but that they differ from the 'mechanical' causality typical of physical phenomena. From this point of view, if we are to be able to explain particular human actions effectively we must gain an understanding of the cultural perspectives on which they are based. That this is necessary is obvious when we are studying a society that is alien to us, since we will find much of what we see and hear puzzling. However, ethnographers argue that it is just as important when we are studying more familiar settings. Indeed, when a setting is familiar the danger of misunderstanding is especially great, since what is observed is so easily

reduced to stereotypes. It is argued that we cannot assume that we already know others' perspectives, even in our own society, because particular groups and individuals develop distinctive worldviews. This is especially true in large, complex societies. Ethnic, occupational, and small informal groups (even individual families or school classes) develop distinctive ways of orienting to the world that may need to be understood if their behaviour is to be explained. Ethnographers argue, then, that it is necessary to learn the culture of the group one is studying before one can produce valid explanations for the behaviour of its members. This is the reason for the centrality of participant observation and unstructured interviewing to ethnography, since these methods promise to provide in-depth understanding of cultural perspectives.[11]

3. *Discovery.* Another feature of ethnographic thinking is a conception of the research process as inductive or discovery-based, rather than as being limited to the testing of explicit hypotheses. It is argued that if one approaches a phenomenon with a set of hypotheses one may fail to discover its true nature, being blinded by the assumptions built into those hypotheses. Instead, one should begin research with minimal assumptions so as to maximise one's capacity for learning. It is for this reason that ethnographers rarely begin their research with specific hypotheses. Rather, they have a general interest in some type of social phenomena and/or in some theoretical issue or practical problem. The focus of the research is narrowed and sharpened, and perhaps even changed substantially, as it proceeds. Similarly, and in parallel, theoretical ideas that frame descriptions and explanations of what is observed are developed over the course of the research. Such ideas are regarded as a valuable outcome of, not a precondition for, research.

These three methodological principles are closely related, indeed they overlap and as I have indicated, they provide the rationale for the specific features of ethnographic method outlined earlier. They are also the basis for much ethnographic criticism of quantitative research for failing to capture the true nature of human social behaviour: because it relies on the study of artificial settings and/or on what people say rather than what they do; because it seeks to reduce meanings to what is 'observable'; and because it reifies social phenomena by treating them as more clearly defined and static than they are, and as mechanical products of social and psychological factors.

In turn, of course, quantitative researchers have questioned the scientific status of ethnography. Let us look briefly at the sort of debate there has been on this issue. Here are some of the criticisms that have been made of ethnographic research, along with the kind of answers given to them by ethnographers.[12]

Criticism: Ethnographic research suffers from a lack of precision as a result of the absence of quantification. For example, words like 'often' and 'frequently' are used instead of more precise numerical specifications. In this way it is impressionistic.

Answer: There is nothing intrinsic to ethnography which rejects quantification, and indeed ethnographic studies do sometimes employ it. However, great precision is not always required. Where differences are large it may be that they can be reported in relatively imprecise ways without loss. Furthermore, there is the danger of overprecision: by insisting on precise quantitative measures we may produce figures that are more precise than we can justify given the nature of the data available, so that the results are misleading. Quantification may also lead to the adoption of measurement techniques that distort what they are intended to capture.

Criticism: Ethnographic observation and interviewing are subjective in the sense that they are not guided by a structure (in the form of a questionnaire or observational schedule) that would maximise the chances that another observer or interviewer would produce similar data. As a result, ethnographic data are peculiarly subject to bias, whose extent cannot be estimated because they are not open to replication.

Answer: It is true that in ethnographic research what data are collected depends on the researcher, and to one degree or another reflects her or his personal characteristics. But all knowledge is personal and cultural in some sense: we cannot escape our social backgrounds and circumstances completely. At the same time, ethnographers use techniques designed to ensure that their findings are not idiosyncratic, for example by comparing data from different sources, a technique sometimes referred to as 'triangulation'. It is also important to note that the structuring of data that quantitative research employs to overcome subjectivity has reactive effects. In other words, people react to the structure itself, thereby increasing the chance that the behaviour studied is an artifact of the research process and is not representative of the phenomena purportedly being described. Nor does the use of schedules solve the problem of subjectivity, because the same structure can be interpreted differently by different people. For example, the same question asked by an interviewer at the same point in an interview may mean different things to different people if they have different perspectives.

Criticism: By studying very small samples ethnographers produce findings that are of little value because they are not generalisable.

Answer: The choice of small samples represents a trade-off between studying cases in depth or in breadth. Ethnography usually sacrifices the latter for the former; survey research does the reverse. And, in sacrificing depth, survey researchers both lose relevant information and run the risk of misunderstanding key features of the cases they study. Moreover, one can make claims about the representativeness of findings without relying on statistical sampling, for example by comparing the features of the case studied with aggregate data about the target population. Equally, one may study a small selection of cases that are designed to represent key dimensions in terms of which the population is assumed to be structured. (It is worth pointing out that social surveys rarely employ pure random sampling; they too rely on assumptions about the 'stratification' of the population.) Furthermore, often, ethnographers are concerned not with empirical generalisation but rather with making theoretical inferences, and this does not necessarily require the case studied to be representative; indeed, extreme cases may be more useful.

Criticism: By studying natural settings and only small samples ethnographers rule out the possibility of physical or statistical control of variables, and as a result they are not able to identify causal relationships.

Answer: Even if causal relationships actually exist in the social world, they are not of the same kind as those in the physical world. Thus, they are not accessible to techniques modelled on investigations in physics. By documenting processes occurring over time, and/or by means of comparative analysis of cases, ethnography is able to trace patterns of relationships among social phenomena in their natural context in a way that neither experiments nor social surveys can do.

Criticism: A key feature of science is the possibility of replication, of other scientists checking the findings of an experiment by repeating it. Since ethnography does not follow a well-designed and explicit procedure that is replicable, its findings cannot be checked by others and are therefore unscientific.

Answer: Replication is not always possible in natural science, and it is not always carried out even when it is possible. This indicates that replication is not the only means by which scientists assess one another's work, and is therefore not an essential feature of science. Nor does it guarantee validity. The fact that it may not be possible in ethnography does not, therefore, detract from the validity of ethnographic findings.

Debates about these issues have gone on for many years, but in some fields in recent times they have largely subsided in favour of a spirit of détente (Rist 1977, Smith and Heshusius 1986). One reason is probably that each side of the quantitative–qualitative divide has become much more heterogeneous, so that other targets for criticism and issues for debate have emerged. Since the 1960s and 1970s, though, when debate about the scientific status of ethnography was at its height in British sociology, there has been a trend toward increased adoption of qualitative method.

Up to now, I have discussed criticisms of ethnography for not being scientific that have come from quantitative researchers. However, there has also been criticism of this kind from *within* the qualitative camp, notably from ethnomethodologists. Their conception of science is influenced by the phenomenological movement in philosophy, which was preoccupied with rigorous explication of the processes by which our perceptions and interpretations of the world are produced. On this basis, ethnomethodologists have been critical of both quantitative and ethnographic research for not living up to the scientific ideal of producing accounts of social phenomena that are rigorously grounded in the analysis of data. Both forms of research are charged with making unexplicated use of commonsense knowledge. In the case of ethnographic research this occurs in the interpretation of people's actions and motives. Ethnomethodologists point out that here cultural knowledge is not just a topic of ethnographic investigation but also a resource used in the analysis, and they regard this as illegitimate. They argue that detailed analysis of the role of commonsense reasoning and knowledge in the way people (including ethnographers) make sense of the world is at the very least an essential first step if social research is to be rigorous. More than this, some ethnomethodologists suggest that because of the context-dependent nature of practical reasoning, it can never provide a foundation for sociological investigation of the kinds of phenomena with which anthropologists and sociologists have conventionally been concerned. Only the study of *practical reasoning itself* is open to rigorous analysis, since such analysis would be self-explicating. What is recommended, then, is a re-specification of the focus of social scientific analysis (Sharrock and Anderson 1986, Button 1991).

In summary, much of the methodological thinking of ethnographers has been shaped by a concern to place their work in relation to natural science and quantitative method. This has often involved attempts to draw a sharp line between ethnography, on the one hand, and journalism and fiction, on the other, despite (or perhaps because of) the similarities. In recent years, however, there has been a noticeable downplaying, if not rejection, of the scientific model on the part of many ethnographers, and increased emphasis on parallels with the humanities. This probably reflects the growth of questioning about the nature and value of science, as well as the rise of interest in literary theory and aesthetics. It has led to criticism of ethnographic work, from inside and outside, for not making a fundamental enough break with the model of natural science and with quantitative method.

Criticisms of ethnography for being too scientific

It is not always easy to tell the difference between criticisms of ethnography for being insufficiently scientific, and criticisms of it for being too scientific. Much depends on the model of science that is being presupposed by the critics. And the past 30 or so years have seen increasing disagreement about the nature of scientific method, along with a trend towards de-emphasising the differences between science and other forms of inquiry and knowledge.

Until the middle of the twentieth century, confidence in scientific method as *the* source of knowledge remained predominant. But, partly as a result of major reconstructions in physics, and demonstrations of the terrible potential of science-based technologies for destruction, this confidence began to be undermined. The philosophy of science in the 1950s experienced the collapse of what had previously been a substantial consensus about the nature of science, founded on logical positivism: that it involved the induction of knowledge from a base of observations that were themselves certain, this process of inference transmitting certainty to the knowledge produced. Questioning of the idea of observational certainties and of the possibility of logical induction was not new, but it increased and its implications came to be taken much more seriously.

Growing doubts about the nature of scientific methodology were symbolised by the impact of Thomas Kuhn's book, *The Structure of Scientific Revolutions*, first published in 1962 (Kuhn 1970). Kuhn argued against views of the history of natural science that portrayed it as a process of cumulative development, achieved by rational investigation that is logically founded on evidence. He showed that the work of the scientists involved in many of the major developments of scientific knowledge of the past was shaped by theoretical assumptions and judgements about the world that were not themselves based on empirical research – some of which are now judged to be false. Kuhn further claimed that the history of science, rather than displaying the gradual build-up of knowledge, is punctuated by periods of revolution when the theoretical assumptions underlying the 'paradigm' in terms of which scientists in a particular field had previously operated are challenged and replaced. (An example is the shift from Newtonian physics to relativity and quantum theory in the early part of the twentieth century.) The replacement of one paradigm by another, according to Kuhn, does not occur on the basis simply of rational assessment of evidence. Paradigms are incommensurable: they picture the world in incompatible ways, so that data themselves are interpreted differently by those working within different paradigms. As a result, paradigm shifts occur as much through representatives of the old paradigm retiring or dying and those of the new one replacing them as by logical argument.[13]

Others have taken these ideas further, for example rejecting the notion of scientific method and the claims of science to produce knowledge (even of the physical world) that is superior to that from other sources, such as religious views (see Feyerabend 1975 and 1978). And today there remains considerable dissensus among philosophers of science; with disagreement, for example, about whether science provides knowledge of reality or simply a record of successful predictions of experience.[14] None of the various attempts to provide an alternative basis for the claim that science is the distinctive source of soundly based knowledge has created a new consensus. One of the effects of this has been to undermine the capacity of natural science to offer a clear model for the social sciences. At the same time, the horrifying capability of science to produce weapons that maim and kill on a massive scale and industries that destroy the environment, has challenged the idea that science represents the spearhead of human progress. Indeed, some commentators have sought to argue that the bitter fruits of scientific work indicate the poisonous nature of the plant (see Passmore 1978).

In this new climate, criticism of ethnography has taken a variety of forms. One target has been the separation of research from practice that it inherits from the scientific model, a criticism reflecting an increased concern with the practical value and consequences of knowledge (Carr and Kemmis 1986, Gitlin *et al.* 1989). Critical theory has been particularly important here, advancing what I will call the 'emancipatory' model. This view of the nature and role of the social sciences derived in large part from the work of the Frankfurt School of Marxism. Jurgen Habermas's early work is probably the most influential presentation of this perspective.[15] He argued that the cognitive interest motivating natural science is that of instrumental control; and that while this is legitimate in the investigation of physical phenomena, it is inappropriate for the study of human behaviour. He claims that this instrumental interest lies behind quantitative social science, and he criticises it for this reason. Habermas regards interpretive research as more appropriate in social science, and believes it to be founded on a concern with overcoming inter-cultural misunderstanding. However, he argues that even this approach is inadequate in the study of advanced capitalist societies because it fails to address the need to emancipate people from ideology, one element of which is the overextension of ideas about knowledge and reality deriving from the natural sciences to our understanding of human social life.

From this perspective, conventional ethnography may be criticised for simply representing things as they are, or for representing them *as they appear to the people studied*. There are two arguments involved here: that ethnography only captures surface appearances, not the underlying reality; and that it is concerned only with documenting current patterns of events or perspectives, not with discovering how these might be *changed* for the better. Critical ethnography, by contrast, sets out to dispel ideology and thereby promote emancipation.

A related development has been the tremendous growth in the influence of feminism, and in particular the attempt to identify aspects of Western thinking, including philosophy and methodology, that betray masculinist bias. The model of the natural sciences and the use of quantitative method have sometimes been criticised as representing such a bias (Graham 1983). There is considerable diversity in feminist thinking about methodology, but an important theme has been a questioning of conventional ethnographic work on similar grounds to critical theorists: that it has been content with mere description rather than being directed towards bringing about emancipation, in this case of women.

An area of special concern to feminists, and to others as well, has been the relationship between researcher and researched, viewed as an aspect of the politics of social research. It has been argued that in more traditional forms of ethnography, as in experimental and survey research, a power relationship is involved. The research is very often focused on relatively powerless groups with the researcher exploiting the latter's powerlessness to carry out the inquiry. And, it is claimed, the research also often serves dominant groups in society, perhaps enabling them to exercise more effective control. From this perspective research itself is seen as a form of domination. Moreover, even where researcher and researched are social equals, power is still involved because it is the researcher who makes the decisions about what is to be studied, how, for what purpose, and so on. It is argued that not only is this unacceptable in itself, but that it distorts the knowledge produced: the findings are often irrelevant to the people being studied, since they are geared to problems defined by social science disciplines, not to those that face the people themselves. Furthermore, research reports are written in language that is not comprehensible to those studied. And such research is often invalid because the ethnographer remains an outsider and fails truly to understand the world from a participant point of view.

Such arguments have been developed in several fields. They are to be found not only among feminists, but also among anthropologists concerned with the role of that discipline in international imperialism; in the field of ethnic relations where the study of ethnic minorities by members of ethnic majorities has been challenged; and also in educational research with the advocacy of 'the teacher as researcher'. The remedy often advocated is participatory research, research by and for participants, with professional researchers playing no more than a facilitative role.[16]

Another way in which the relevance of the scientific model to ethnography has been challenged focuses on ethnographers' claims that their accounts represent reality. As we saw, one of the rationales for ethnography has been that it can capture the nature of human social life more accurately than quantitative methods. This is a key element of the ethnographic commitment to 'naturalism' and 'discovery'. However, some critics (including some ethnographers) argue that any such appeal to the representation of reality is ill-founded. Such questioning of the representational capacity of ethnography can arise simply from applying the concept of understanding to the research process itself: if it is true that people construct interpretations of the world, and that different groups and individuals construct *different* perspectives, then we may be led to conclude that this is also true of ethnographers, and that the accounts produced by them are simply one version of the world that is no more valid than others. This tendency towards rejection of the possibility of representation (which I will call anti-realism) has also been reinforced by the influence of a wide range of philosophical ideas, including phenomenology, hermeneutics, structuralism and Wittgensteinian language philosophy.[17]

Most recently, anti-realism has been encouraged by the influence of post-structuralism and post-modernism, notably the work of Derrida, Foucault and Lyotard. Despite very important differences among these writers, a central theme in their work is rejection of the possibility of a single true understanding of the world. Thus, Derrida emphasises the instability of meaning in discourse, Lyotard the diversity and incommensurability of language games, and Foucault the role of power in constituting what counts as knowledge in different historical periods. Indeed, the work of the latter is specifically concerned with exposing the role of medical, psychological and social science in the exercise of social control. It is under the influence of these philosophical trends that criticism of the role of social research in society has increasingly been combined with an epistemological critique of its foundations.[18]

One of the effects of the growing influence of anti-realism has been increased scrutiny of ethnographic and other accounts *as texts*, looking at the rhetorical devices that are used to 'create' the world portrayed. The suggestion is that conventional ethnographic work is wedded to a spurious literary realism: it claims to represent the setting studied 'as it is', but this is not possible because we have no access to an independent reality, all we have are interpretations; and the ethnographer's account is just as much an interpretation as those of the people that he or she is studying. These critics claim that, in order to establish that their accounts represent reality, ethnographers rely on rhetorical devices that are analogous to those employed by travel writers and realist novelists such as Dickens or Zola. For example, anthropologists sometimes include in their accounts a description of their first sight of the setting they were to study, thereby 'proving' in a narrative way that they have 'really' been there and have seen what they report. Similarly, one finds superfluous details in ethnographic accounts, information that is not necessary to support the analysis. This is included, it is suggested, to give an added sense of realism to the account, just as novelists like Dickens spend much time describing the details of the settings in which events take place, as well as the appearance and manner of the people involved.[19]

Not all of those who have been concerned with the rhetorical strategies employed by ethnographers have adopted an anti-realist position, but many have. Of course, these critics do not reject the use of rhetorical devices, they argue that rhetoric cannot be avoided. But they do reject rhetorical strategies which, as they see it, pretend to an unattainable realism. Instead, they claim that research is a form of story-telling, and argue that it should give voice to those they see as marginalised by white, middle-class, male culture. Such arguments have motivated novel kinds of ethnographic writing, for example texts that incorporate the voices of the people studied in a more substantial and less controlled way than is common in conventional ethnographic accounts.[20]

From a variety of points of view, then, conventional ethnographic research has come under criticism in recent times, not so much for failing to be scientific but for still seeking to adopt the scientific model. Its commitment to describing and explaining the social world, rather than trying to change it, has also been rejected by some. And the relationship between ethnography and the people studied has sometimes been attacked as exploitative. Finally, ethnography's very capacity to represent social reality 'in its own terms' has been challenged.

Conclusion

In this chapter I have outlined the character of ethnography as a set of research strategies as well as the more philosophical ideas that support those strategies. In addition, I have looked at methodological debates about ethnography, both those concerned with criticism that it is not scientific enough and those centred on arguments that the model of natural science is inappropriate for ethnography.

If what I have said makes it sound as if ethnography is currently in crisis, this is not far from the truth. Most obvious is the crisis of fragmentation: there is no single ethnographic paradigm or community, but a diversity of approaches claiming to be ethnographic (whose proponents often disagree with one another). More fundamentally, though, the crisis stems from deep, unresolved questions about the possibility and nature of our knowledge of the social world and about the purposes which research can and should serve. Of course, these questions face *all* social and educational researchers, not just ethnographers. Ethnographers are struggling with them, but there is little agreement about solutions.

What is presented in the remainder of this book represents one attempt to deal with some of these problems in the context of providing a guide to reading ethnographic research. It is necessarily tentative, and controversial. In the next chapter I begin by looking at how we should set about understanding the claims made in ethnographic texts.

Notes

1. In this book I shall use 'ethnography' in a wide sense that is largely synonymous with 'qualitative method'. This has become an increasingly common usage, and it is justified to some extent by the fact that there is little agreement over competing narrower definitions of the term.
2. For a brief overview of the history of ethnography in the context of social and cultural anthropology, see Wax (1971). Stocking (1996) provides a more detailed intellectual history, one which stresses continuities rather than discontinuities. For a history of twentieth century Anglo-American sociology that focuses on methodological approaches, see Madge (1962). Burgess (1982:ch. 1) provides a useful brief account of the recent history of ethnography in both anthropology and sociology. See also Vidich and Lyman (1995).
3. Malinowski was not the only figure in this movement, nor did his research practice always conform very closely to the ethnographic ideal that he recommended. See Kaberry (1957) and Wax (1972).
4. For detailed discussions of the Chicago School, see Bulmer (1984) and Harvey (1987).
5. For accounts of the US and British traditions of community study, see Bell and Newby (1971). Stein (1960) and Frankenberg (1966) provide systematic presentations of some of the findings. See also Cole (1977) on the anthropology of European society. On the Lynds, see Madge (1962:ch. 5) and Vidich and Lyman (1995).
6. For examples of this research, see Whyte (1981), Rose (1962), Becker *et al.* (1961 and 1969). For attempts to codify and develop ethnographic method in this period, see Glaser and Strauss (1967), McCall and Simmons (1969), and Becker (1970).
7. For brief histories of qualitative research in Britain, see Payne *et al.* (1981) and Strong (1988). Atkinson *et al.* (1988) provide a review of British qualitative research on education.
8. See the discussion in Bryman (1988).
9. For an example of this type of argument, see Smith (1989).
10. Use of the term 'naturalism' is ambiguous in the methodological literature. It is sometimes employed to refer to the adoption of the natural science model, sometimes (as here) to indicate a concern with capturing the *nature* of the phenomena studied (which may well imply using different methods to those characteristic of the natural sciences). See Matza (1969) for a discussion of the term and references to its diversity of usage. For clear accounts of the covering law model, see Lessnoff (1974) and Keat and Urry (1975). On the pattern model of explanation, see the discussion and references in Hammersley (1989).
11. It should be said, though, that ethnographers do not believe that understanding requires that they become full members of the group(s) being studied. Indeed, most believe that this must not occur if a valid and useful account is to be produced. The ethnographer should try to be both outsider and insider, staying on the margins of the group both socially and intellectually.
12. I cannot cover the full range of criticism and response; the aim is simply to give a flavour of the sort of argument and counter-argument that has taken place. I am also not intending to endorse either the criticisms or the defences. The issues involved are often more complex and difficult than such exchanges suggest, and I will discuss some of them in more detail later.

13. Kuhn did not deny the role of rational judgement, simply that it provided the sole and certain basis for paradigm shift. (See, especially, the postscript to the second edition of his book: Kuhn 1970.)

14. For reviews of these arguments, and references, see Siegel (1987), Tiles (1988), and Newton-Smith (1990).

15. See Habermas (1987) and Fay (1975). For an overview of Habermas's work, see McCarthy (1978).

16. For assessments of the arguments for critical ethnography, feminist methodology and practitioner research, see Hammersley (1992 and 1995a).

17. While these ideas differ in many ways and are by no means all straightforwardly anti-realist, collectively their influence has encouraged anti-realism in sociology. For a useful introductory discussion of these intellectual movements, see Anderson *et al.* (1986).

18. For useful accounts of post-structuralism and post-modernism, see Dews (1987) and Docherty (1992).

19. For these arguments about the textual construction of reality by anthropologists and sociologists, see Clifford (1983), Clifford and Marcus (1986), Marcus and Fischer (1986), Geertz (1988), van Maanen (1988), Atkinson (1990 and 1992).

20. See, for example, Krieger (1983), Shostak (1981) and Crapanzano (1980). For an extended discussion of these developments, see Denzin (1997).

Understanding ethnographic accounts

We may read ethnographic studies for a variety of reasons, but for most purposes a first requirement is that we understand what knowledge claims the author is making, and on what grounds. These may seem a relatively straightforward matter, fixed in black and white on the page before us. But what is on the page is simply print. To get at what we are interested in we have to *interpret* what is written. And, as we shall see, this is not always a simple matter. Moreover, some of the reasons for this lie in the forms that ethnographic texts take.

Modes of ethnographic writing

There is no standard format of presentation for ethnographic research reports. They rarely follow the structure that is recommended for quantitative reports: presentation of the research problem and hypotheses; account of the methods employed; statement of the findings; discussion of the implications of these. Instead, formats vary greatly, often being organised around key themes that have emerged during the analysis; relating, for example, to the different perspectives of the main participants, the phases through which their activities or experience passes, and so on.

As noted in the previous chapter, in recent years the nature of ethnographic texts has been given increasing attention.[1] Thus, ethnographers have become more self-conscious about the way they write, and the assumptions about knowledge and the world this involves. One of the fruits of this new self-consciousness has been the identification of various modes of ethnographic writing, some of which may occur within the same text. The commonest form is what is referred to as ethnographic 'realism' or 'naturalism'.[2] Here, the account is written in such a way as to give readers the impression that they are observing the scene described. The researcher is often absent from these portrayals, as if he or she were merely a camera. Here is van Maanen's summary description of this form of writing:

Basically, the narrator of realist tales poses as an impersonal conduit who, unlike missionaries, administrators, journalists, or unabashed members of the culture themselves, passes on more-or-less objective data in a measured intellectual style that is uncontaminated by personal bias, political goals, or moral judgments.

(van Maanen 1988:47)

Van Maanen notes that such writing includes 'precise, mundane details', takes account of the 'native point of view' by including quotations from informants, but maintains the researcher's 'interpretive omnipotence' in that he or she 'has the last word'.

This sort of ethnographic writing is often very close in character to that which is typical of histories, biographies, and even novels. Here is an example:

At the end of Winston Street is a yellow wall with a number of graffiti – a list of boys, *Jimmy, Norman, Eddie, Marvin, Robert*, and a list of girls next to it, *Barbie, Debbie, Sarah, Peaches, Janice*. There is a secretive *Leroy loves somebody*, and a couple of four-letter words scrawled by an uncertain hand. A little to the side, the message is that *Your mother drink wild irish rose*, with the reply *So do your cat*. Wild Irish Rose is the drink of the winos, 'wineheads' or 'juiceheads' in ghetto parlance.

Winston Street, Washington D.C., is a narrow, one-way ghetto street, one block long and lined by brick row houses, two or three stories high and in varying states of repair. In the windows of some of them are flower pots, bright curtains or even venetian blinds. Others have broken blinds, dirty plastic sheets, or nothing at all. Sometimes a house is condemned as unfit to live in, and its doors and windows are covered with boards. It is largely a residential street, and, since it is not really a thoroughfare, its pedestrian and auto traffic is largely confined to the street's own residents and their visitors. At the corners of Winston Street and the surrounding streets are small business establishments: groceries, liquor stores, carry-out food shops, variety stores, laundromats, shoeshine shops, barber shops, beauty salons; all very modest in appearance. These are the establishments which cater to the day-to-day needs, and supply the few luxuries, of ghetto living. The consumption of liquor is considerable. The carry-outs find most of their customers among the many single men who cannot prepare food in their rented rooms, as well as among the children and adolescents who spend much of whatever money they can get on extra food and goodies. Variety stores sell candy, school equipment, cheap toys, and a variety of other inexpensive odds and ends. The carry-outs, the barber shops, and the shoeshine shops serve not only their manifest function but are also the hangouts, the centers of sociability, of teenagers and adult men. To serve as locales of leisure, they add some more items to their furnishings: newspapers, vending machines for cigarettes and soft drinks, a pinball machine, a juke box, a public telephone. No one establishment would have them all, some would have none of this, but many have some of it ...

(Hannerz 1969:19)

These are the opening paragraphs of the first chapter of Ulf Hannerz's ethnographic classic *Soulside*, a study of black community life in Washington D.C. carried out in the late 1960s. Extracts like this abound in ethnographies, especially where the setting investigated is being first introduced. However, most naturalistic writing is not as concretely descriptive as this. The central goal of ethnographic research is often conceptualised as providing an analytic, theoretical, or 'thick' description, rather than just the relatively concrete, commonsensical kind illustrated above. Such descriptions (whether of whole societies, small communities, organisations, spatial locations, or 'social worlds') must not only remain close to the concrete reality of particular events, but also reveal general features of the life of a particular category of people, group or setting, or even of human social life as a whole. As the terminology implies, 'theoretical descriptions' claim to be simultaneously descriptions and theories, and their theoretical elements cannot be extracted from them without coming to seem 'commonplace and vacant' (Geertz 1973:25). Theoretical descriptions are, then, laced with reflections about the significance of what is described.

Hannerz provides such theoretical description later on in his book. For example, he presents some examples of conversations among men hanging out on streetcorners, and in seeking to understand these he draws on a variety of theoretical and empirical literature in order to highlight similarities and differences between these conversations and those characteristic of, for example, middle-class parties. Here is a brief illustration:

The men seem preoccupied with creating and maintaining a definition of natural masculinity which they can all share. By seizing on individual experiences of kinds which they have all had, they 'talk through' and thereby construct the social reality of the typical Ghetto Man, a fact of life larger than any one of them. This Ghetto Man is a bit of a hero, a bit of a villain, and a bit of a fool, yet none of them all the way. He is in fact a kind of a trickster – uncertainty personified, a creature fluctuating between competence and incompetence, success and failure, good and evil. He applies his mother wit or is plainly lucky sometimes ... and this helps him come out victorious or at least unscathed. But not all the time, for native wit and luck have their limits...

Anyway, when Ghetto Man succeeds, he is a hero, considering his limited skills and powers in an environment full of adversaries; if he fails it is natural because he was up to no good.

(Hannerz 1969:112)

What Hannerz presents here is an interpretation of the stories exchanged by the streetcorner men he observed, drawing out what he takes their significance to be for the nature of men's lives in the ghetto. Often theoretical descriptions involve the categorisation of the phenomena described under some general concept or set of concepts, perhaps one that is novel to the account. Thus, Hannerz refers to the story-telling he describes as 'mythmaking', something that we can expect to find in other settings as well.[3] In these ways, theoretical hypotheses, interpretations and conclusions are woven into the account as part of the description.

Ethnographic accounts rarely, if ever, consist solely of naturalistic writing of these kinds. At some point, often near the beginning, there will usually be discussion of the focus of the research, why it is of significance, what methods were employed and so on. And at the end there may be a summary of the findings and some conclusions. We can refer to this as expository writing, in which the author locates his or her work in an appropriate context and discusses the implications that can be drawn from it. As we shall see later in this chapter, this mode of writing can be an important source of the information that is necessary for assessing ethnographic research.

There is an additional form of writing that has become popular among ethnographers in recent years: what has been called the 'confessional' mode, in which the 'inside story' of the research is told. The anthropologist Clifford Geertz refers to this as 'the diary disease', so popular has it become (Geertz 1988:90). In its fully developed form the confessional mode may include reports of incidents that are potentially discrediting for the researcher; though the effect is usually to show that the researcher had direct contact with the people and settings he or she describes. In one of the earliest examples of this genre William Foote Whyte reports his naivety at the start of his research on an Italian area in Boston, USA in the late 1930s, and his later participation in election-rigging (Whyte 1993). More recently, in writing about his research on an institution for the 'mentally retarded', the sociologist Steven Taylor reports how he witnessed abuse of residents and discusses the dilemma this created (Taylor 1991:245–6). Of course, while such confessional accounts purport to give the inside story of the research, they are always selective. What is included depends on what the writer judges to be relevant (and on what he or she is prepared to admit!). Also, they are accounts from one particular point of view, that of the researcher. Nevertheless, such research biographies offer information about the researcher and the course of inquiry that may not be available elsewhere, and which can be helpful in assessing research findings.

The naturalistic, expository and confessional forms of writing are the most common ones to be found in ethnographic accounts. The first two are present in most ethnographies, with the naturalistic mode usually predominating. More confessional writing may also be present, though research biographies are often published separately from the study to which they relate. It is worth noting that there are some other, more unusual, kinds of ethnographic writing. Van Maanen refers to 'impressionist tales', taking the form of dramatic recall. There is also writing that departs from naturalism by abandoning the voice of a narrator. Krieger's (1983) study of a women's community is an example of this. Her whole account consists of the words of the women themselves, derived from interviews and reported in indirect speech. There have also been novel approaches in life history work. Crapanzano (1980), for example, presents the life history of Tuhami, an illiterate Moroccan tile maker, doing this in such a way as to try to avoid what he sees as the tendency of conventional ethnography to 'render bizarre, exotic, or downright irrational what would have been ordinary in its own context' (p. 8). This requires paying attention both to the rhetorical devices by which Tuhami tells his stories and to those that Crapanzano himself employs to locate them; as well as to the active role that the latter played in eliciting the life history. Crapanzano asks his readers 'to abandon for the moment [their] assumptions about reality' so that they will share 'some of the anguished puzzlement I felt, and presumably Tuhami felt, as we tried to make sense of each other' (Crapanzano 1980:23). In addition, there are studies that employ the technique of collage (Dorst 1989, Rose 1989), and there are some ethnographers who have resorted to poetry (Richardson 1993, Johnson 1993).[4]

I shall not give these unconventional modes of presentation much attention, since they are still relatively rare. However, it is important to recognise the criticisms of the more conventional modes of writing that have motivated them. The mix of naturalistic and expository writing that makes up most ethnographic accounts is closely wedded to the three assumptions that I identified as basic to ethnography in Chapter 1; and it is some aspects of those assumptions that advocates of these new approaches challenge. Central here, as I noted in Chapter 1, is rejection of ethnographers' claims to describe phenomena that are independent of them. In laying the basis for his analysis of the textual strategies used by ethnographers, van Maanen illustrates this anti-realism. He comments that: 'culture is not strictly speaking a scientific object, but is created, as is the reader's view of it, by the active construction of a text' (van Maanen 1988:7). While I do not accept this anti-realism, there is no doubt that it points to an important problem facing conventional ethnography (Hammersley 1992:ch. 1). The naturalistic mode of writing tends to portray communities, settings and people without explicit indication of the framework of relevances on which the description was based, or of its purpose. The implication which follows from this mode of writing is that what is provided is a more or less accurate reproduction of the phenomena described. And there are several reasons to question this implication.

First, it is never possible to reproduce a phenomenon by describing it. Descriptions are always selective: they focus on some aspects of phenomena and omit others. As a result, there are always multiple, non-contradictory, true accounts possible of any scene. Given the selective character of ethnographic description, we need to know the basis for selection. Ethnographic descriptions in the naturalistic mode typically do not make this explicit, and associated expository writing does not always compensate for this.

Second, naturalism effectively assumes that validity of descriptions can be ensured by close contact with the phenomenon being described. Thus, ethnographic writing is often preoccupied with establishing that the ethnographer has been to the place and seen what is described. As Geertz remarks about anthropological ethnography:

> the ability of anthropologists to get us to take what they say seriously [has to do] ... with their capacity to convince us that what they say is a result of their having actually penetrated (or, if you prefer, having been penetrated by) another form of life, of having ... truly 'been there'.
>
> (Geertz 1988:4 5)

Van Maanen refers to this as the 'doctrine of immaculate perception' (van Maanen 1988:74); and, as the pun implies, this form of legitimation is weak. Witnesses to the same events are quite capable of producing contradictory accounts. Indeed, the principle of understanding implies that people from different cultures are very likely to do this. While first-hand observation and contact with what is being described will greatly aid accurate description, it by no means guarantees it. Furthermore, it is worth remembering that what is included in ethnographic research reports is not simply what the researcher experienced but an interpretation and development of that experience. Indeed, much that is described by ethnographers cannot have been *seen* or *heard* in any straightforward way. What ethnographers 'discover' in the course of fieldwork is a product of complex processes of understanding, as well as of social interaction between themselves and the various people participating in the setting observed, including those acting as their informants. It is never a simple reflection of what exists.

Thus, ethnographic naturalism can be systematically misleading, and this highlights the need for careful reading of ethnographic texts. If we read such accounts in a relatively passive way, we may be lulled into accepting what they portray at face value. A more careful, and more questioning, approach to reading is necessary if we are to understand them effectively.

A strategy for reading

To start with, we must be clear about what it is that we are trying to understand. My focus is the accounts produced by research, not the research processes that generated them.[5] A single research project may produce several research reports, for example articles focusing on various aspects of the phenomenon investigated, perhaps a book, perhaps also a research biography. Furthermore, because of the exploratory and developmental character of ethnography, there may be a difference between the original focus of the research and the focus of the report(s) it produces. Equally, there may be a discrepancy between the terms in which the research focus is justified and the motives that originally inspired the research. For example, Punch (1979) justifies his focus on policing in a central area of Amsterdam on the general grounds that the problems facing the police in metropolitan city centres have been largely ignored by Anglo-American work, and that there is virtually no Dutch research on policing at all. However, his more confessional discussion of how his research came to be located in Amsterdam reveals the element of contingency frequently to be found in the selection of ethnographic research topics and sites. He reports his failure to get permission to study the police in Britain, mentions that he had spent some time in The Netherlands on a research fellowship and that his wife is Dutch. And he comments that his interest in Amsterdam's city centre stemmed from his knowledge that police stations there would be busy:

Given my limited time, I wanted to observe as much as possible and had little inclination to spend my time in a sleepy suburb with traffic accidents and violations as the major diversions from tedium and drinking coffee.
(Punch 1979:3)

As this example illustrates, information about the research process is relevant to assessing the research reports it produces. And it will usually be worthwhile to look at other accounts deriving from the same research (and especially any research biography) if these are available. However, these are useful only insofar as they illuminate the account(s) we are trying to understand.

In reading an ethnographic account it is important to distinguish among various aspects of it that serve different functions. The main aspects are: the research focus; the case(s) studied; the methods of data collection and analysis used; the major claims and the evidence provided for them; and, finally, the conclusions drawn about the research focus. These elements are not always clearly indicated or differentiated by ethnographic writers, but information about all of them is essential.

The research focus

I will use the term 'research focus' to refer to the most general set of phenomena (one or more) about which a study makes claims, and the aspects of it that are of concern. For instance, the focus of Hannerz's *Soulside* is various features of the culture of black communities in the United States, plus some of the causes and consequences of these.

More specifically, we can think of the research focus as the general set of questions that a study addresses. And, it is important to distinguish between the different sorts of question that might be addressed. These can be descriptive, explanatory, or theoretical, and may even be evaluative or prescriptive. The distinctions among these types of question are not always observed by ethnographers and thus are often not clearly marked in ethnographic texts. Indeed, as I noted earlier, ethnographic work is frequently guided by the notion of theoretical description, which in effect seeks to combine description, explanation and theory; sometimes incorporating evaluative and prescriptive elements too. However, in my view it is important to recognise the diversity of product to be found among ethnographic accounts, not least because the different types of claim place varying requirements on the researcher, in terms of the sort of evidence that is required to support them, and they therefore have implications for what evidence the reader should expect. Of course, a study may aim at more than one type of product, in which case we must interpret it in terms of the requirements implied by all of its goals.

Besides the focus itself, we must also look out for any rationale that the author offers as to why it is important, and thus why the conclusions might be of interest to us. An example is provided in the Introduction to *Soulside*, where Hannerz notes that a considerable amount of social science research has been done on black communities, but claims that as a result of its character it has been largely ignored. He reports the complaints of some black critics that such research has failed to capture the nature of ghetto life. Indeed, he notes how those wishing to understand the experience of black people living in the USA often turn to novels and poetry rather than to the work of social scientists. Against this background, he suggests that:

> perhaps anthropology [by which in this context he can be taken to mean ethnography] can give a more insightful picture of [the] human side to the ghetto condition than other social sciences do. The willfulness, endurance, strength and humanity ... can be understood only within the grassroots context, and anthropology as a form of consciousness may be better able to inquire into these personal terms of life while at the same time remaining more systematic than the literary view of the black experience.
> (Hannerz 1969:14).[6]

Most ethnographic accounts provide some explicit statement of their focus and of the assumed significance of the study. Usually this occurs at the beginning of the account; though it need not occur *right* at the start, and relevant material may be found in any part of a research report and in other sources too.

In book-length studies the rationale for the research focus may amount to one or more chapters, including reviews of the literature which identify the gap that the study is intended to fill. As another illustration of the sorts of information that may be provided about focus and rationale, here is an example taken from Strong's book *The Ceremonial Order of the Clinic*:

> This is a book about the meetings that doctors have with parents when a child is sick or needs medical inspection. ... It says nothing about the medicine involved in all this and very little about people's feelings, opinions or perceptions. These things are interesting but they are not my interest here. My concern is with ceremonies: with the social form of the occasion and the sorts of identity tacitly claimed by each party and conferred upon the other.
>
> ... The point of my description is this: here are over a thousand separate occasions on which parents met doctors and met them in all kinds of different circumstances, and yet the manner of their meeting, the ceremonial order of the occasion, was pretty much the same no matter what other things might vary. One can go further. The outward form of their relationship took just the one shape, give or take a few minor alterations, in all of the Scottish consultations and in most of the American ones too.
>
> So here we have something fairly powerful, a manner of meeting, a mode of being doctor and parent, which was used across a great range of contingencies and particularities; this mode – the 'bureaucratic format' – is

my main topic and I shall try to describe its nature, its origins, the methods by which it was sustained and the actual fit between this outward show and the matters which it clothed.

In doing all this I have several aims, some modest, others less so. One is to comment on medical work with children and their parents, another is to reflect more generally on medical consultations, for although paediatrics is one small segment of the clinical world its methods and dilemmas may well have their counterparts in other areas of medicine. There may also be something for sociologists. Medical consultations are merely one in a myriad of those occasions and events which sociologists study, and the frames or formats used therein may be of little interest save to specialists in the field of service relationships. Nevertheless, since the master of ceremony, Erving Goffman himself, has paid little attention to the study of any one order, the careful delineation of a form may still have something to say about formats in general and the structures which shape our daily lives.

(Strong 1979:ix–x)

Statements like this are not always immediately accessible. They assume background knowledge (in this case, for instance, about who Erving Goffman is and what 'ceremonial order' might mean). Like all writing, they are directed at a particular audience about whom assumptions regarding knowledge and interest are made, and it may be that as readers we do not match those assumptions. However, even though parts of what the author writes may be obscure to us we will usually be able to get the gist of what is being focused on, the sort of questions that are being asked, and why.

Strong gives some indication of the focus of his study in the very first sentence that I quoted: '...meetings that doctors have with parents when a child is sick or needs medical inspection'. The remainder of that first paragraph spells out the aspect of this phenomenon in which he is interested: his account is designed to answer the questions, 'what is the social form of the occasion?', and 'what sorts of identity are claimed by each party and are conferred on the other?'. And we can note that these seem to be descriptive questions.

The next two paragraphs of the extract are confusing from our point of view, since they seem to summarise one of the findings of the study (that the 'bureaucratic format' was the dominant one). Such mixing of focus and findings is not uncommon in ethnographic studies, so that sometimes it is not easy to tell what belongs where. But, as far as is possible, it is worth keeping them apart.

The final paragraph of the extract from Strong's book hints at the rationale for the focus of his study, but in doing so it complicates the identification of focus that we made on the basis of the first paragraph. The object that we identified earlier (medical work with children and their parents) is now itself subsumed under the headings of three broader foci: medical consultations of all kinds, service relationships, and (implicitly) human relationships in general. Ethnographic studies can have more than one focus, then, and identifying these may require careful reading. In subsequent analysis attention will need to be given to how well the study addresses each of its foci. We should note that the rationales for these different foci may also differ. Thus, in the conclusion to his book Strong presents both practical recommendations about how paediatric consultations might be improved as well as conclusions relating to the theoretical literature dealing with interactional formats of all kinds. His study, therefore, has both practical and theoretical rationales.

What I have quoted from Strong's study is only a small part of a lengthy process of scene-setting. This takes up not only the Preface (from which the extract comes) but also the first chapter, in which he discusses other literature dealing with contacts between staff and patients, pointing out that it neglects the features he is concerned with and outlining what he takes to be the consequences of this.

In summary, then, the first task in seeking to understand an ethnographic text is to identify the focus, or foci, of the research and any accompanying rationale. The next is to identify the case(s) investigated.

The case(s) studied

We need to be careful in distinguishing the focus of the research from the case or cases studied. I defined the focus above as the most general set of phenomena about which the study makes claims. Usually, this will be a type of phenomena or some large aggregate of cases. Examples already mentioned include: black communities in US cities, paediatric consultations, and service encounters. By 'the case(s) studied', on the other hand, I mean the phenomena specifically located in place and time about which data were collected. For example, while Hannerz drew conclusions about black community life in general, his data relate to the people of Winston Street, Washington D.C. during some period in the 1960s. So, black culture was his focus, and the Winston Street community at that time was his case. Interestingly, Duneier's more recent study has a similar focus, but he produces a rather different picture as a result of investigating a contrasting case: a group of men, in employment or retired, who frequent a restaurant in a mixed area of Chicago (Duneier 1992).

I noted in Chapter 1 that ethnographic research typically investigates a small number of cases, often only one. In this respect Hannerz's and Duneier's studies are typical. Strong's study of medical encounters, on the other hand, is unusual since his analysis is based on data from 1,120 encounters between doctors and parents. Obviously, the smaller the size of the case the more examples can be studied with the same resources (other things being equal), but such a large number of cases is rare in ethnographic research.

It is worth noting that ethnographic accounts often intermingle discussion of focus and case. An example is Atkinson's account of the clinical years of the medical education of doctors, where the writing moves at will between the focus (the experiences and perspectives of medical students in general) and the sample of Edinburgh medical students that Atkinson studied in the early 1970s. Even so, it is usually relatively straightforward to distinguish between focus and case, not least because the former is generally of significance for a wide audience, whereas the latter is not. I doubt whether many of us are interested, for its own sake, in information about the lives of the Winston Street inhabitants of the 1960s (Hannerz 1969) or about some Edinburgh medical students in the 1970s (Atkinson 1981a) or about the clientele of the Valois cafe in Chicago in the late 1980s (Duneier 1992). Whatever interest we have stems from what we may infer from this information, for example about black community life or medical students in more general terms.

There are exceptions to this, of course. If it is true that the 'Doomsday Cult' that Lofland studied in the early 1960s was one of the seed groups of the Moonies (Lynch 1977), then it may have intrinsic interest over and above what Lofland is able to tell us about cults in general (Lofland 1966). Much the same applies to Nigel Fielding's study of the English far right group the National Front in the 1970s. He presents his study as an investigation of political deviance and discusses the criteria for selecting a group to investigate this topic. However, a study of the National Front (even though limited in time-span, and now out of date) is of general interest in itself, as Fielding recognises: 'This party meets my criteria for a political group whose study can contribute to an understanding of ... political deviance while also being worthy of description and analysis in its own right' (Fielding 1981:7). For the most part, though, the cases studied by ethnographers are of rather limited interest in themselves (even though they are or were of great interest to the people involved). And usually, of course, their identity is disguised from readers through the use of pseudonyms, so that we cannot easily identify the actual case(s) studied.

Sometimes the focus of the research may apparently be restricted to the case(s) that have been studied even though these are not of obvious general interest. For example, some of my own work explicitly limits its claims to what occurred in a particular inner-city secondary modern school in Northern England in the early 1970s (Hammersley 1974). Such a cautious limitation of focus is naive, it now seems to me. After all, why would my study warrant publication if it did not have implications for some wider focus? In such cases I think we must conclude that, in effect, the focus is different to the case studied, but is left implicit. Where this occurs, we need to identify what seems likely to have been the intended focus, or what can reasonably be treated as the focus.

Most accounts provide at least some information about the case(s) selected and the reasons for their selection; and further information may be obtained from other sources, notably research biographies. Of course, the information that could be provided is virtually endless. What it is necessary to know depends on the focus of the research and on our familiarity with similar cases. Thus, a study of primary school classrooms does not need to give most British readers much information about the setting. Here is the information that is provided in a study of gender imbalances in such classrooms:

The data to be considered comprise a verbatim transcription of a fourth-year junior school lesson (pupils aged 10 and 11 years). The lesson is one from an extended series that one of us (JF) observed and recorded as part of an ethnographic study of gender differentiation in primary classrooms. ... The lesson is organized as a teacher–class discussion of the topic 'What I do on Mondays and what I would like to do on Mondays'. In an earlier lesson pupils had addressed this topic in writing, but their essay answers proved unsatisfactory to the teacher. The present lesson therefore covers a number of points which, the teacher explains, he would like to have seen included. After the lesson, pupils make a second attempt at the essay. The class contained 29 pupils, 16 girls and 13 boys. The teacher was male.

(French and French 1984:128)

By contrast, an article on dock pilferage by longshoremen in St Johns, Newfoundland provides over five pages of description of the port and the different types of work in which longshoremen (or dock workers) are involved (Mars 1974); it is probably true that such information is required if most British (and probably even most Canadian) readers are to be able to understand the findings.

In addition to information about the case(s) studied, we must also look out for any indication of why these are believed to provide a basis for investigating the research focus, and how they were selected. This may involve the claim that what was studied is typical of some type or population of cases. For example, Westley justifies the case he studied in his investigation of police violence as follows:

The police department was located in a small mid-western industrial city. At the time of the study this city seemed similar to large urban centers in having a slum area, a sizable Negro sub-community, major traffic problems, a system of political patronage, and a high crime rate. This city was not, of course, representative of major urban centers in the United States for its size, economic composition, and political influence sharply differentiated it from them. But as far as the police are concerned, it posed most of the major problems encountered by police departments in the larger cities in traffic, in political corruption, in crime, in ethnic relations, and so forth. Its policemen reacted as if they were urban policemen.

(Westley 1970:xi–xii)

Westley seems to be arguing here that the city he studied was typical of others in most respects that are important for the generalisation of his findings, even though it is also atypical in some ways.

Alternatively, cases are sometimes justified precisely on the basis of their atypicality. Cicourel and Kitsuse (1973) studied Lakeside High, a school that they point out was unrepresentative of US high schools at the time, not just in serving an exclusively high income neighborhood but also in its large size, bureaucratic structure and professionalised counselling service. However, they argue that this school was in the vanguard of changes that were taking place among US high schools so that more and more schools would become similar to Lakeside High in respects relevant to their research findings. On this basis, they claim that their findings will be generalisable to many other schools in the future. This amounts to generalising about what *will* happen, and it has also been argued that qualitative research can also illuminate what are future *possibilities* as well as probabilities, for example investigating cases that approximate to some ideal (Schofield 1990).

As we shall see, the question of the relationship between case and focus is complex; I will discuss this further when looking at conclusions below.

Methods used

Having identified the research focus, the case(s) studied and the rationales for them, the next task is to look at the means by which the investigation was carried out: what sources of data were employed; what were the relationships between the researcher and the people studied; what analytic techniques were used, and so on.

As I noted in Chapter 1, it is characteristic of ethnography to employ a range of data sources: fieldnotes from observation and perhaps also from participation; audio- and video-recordings and transcripts; interviews; documents; and perhaps also questionnaire responses and/or test results. But even this range of types of data does not reveal the full potential variation.

Observation, for example, can take a variety of forms (Foster 1996). It may be covert or overt, to different degrees and varying in relation to the participants involved; and it may involve participation in an established role in the setting (marginal or more central) or as a 'visitor' or in a specially created researcher role. At one extreme, for example, there is the covert research of Melville Dalton reported in *Men Who Manage*, where only a few of the people in the settings where he took work knew that he was also carrying out research, and even they knew little about it (Dalton 1959). At the other end of the spectrum is the already mentioned research of the Swede Ulf Hannerz in a black community in America, a man whose very appearance and accent would presumably have marked him out for everyone as a visitor.

Observation can also vary in the degree to which it relies on pre-defined categories. While ethnographers usually employ an 'unstructured' approach, on occasion they may engage in more structured observation. For example, in an ethnographic study of the early years of schooling, Rist used 'systematic' observation yielding quantitative data at one point, in an attempt to document the differential treatment of the children (Rist 1970).

Interviewing can also vary in the degree to which the interviewer structures the interaction, how directive the questions are, and so on. Sometimes ethnographers use relatively structured interviews, similar in form to those characteristic of survey research, in order to gain the same information from a large number of participants. More commonly, ethnographic interviews are open-ended, designed to explore the perspectives of the people concerned. However, even within such exploratory interviews there may be some directive questions designed to test responses or even to provoke.[7]

Documents may also vary in character. They may be elicited by the researcher or may have been produced for other purposes. And extant documents include personal diaries and letters as well as public documents like official reports or commercially published books. How documents were produced, by whom, for what purposes, with what audience in mind, and so on, can have important consequences for how they can be used as evidence.

In short, the character of the data employed may have implications for the kinds of threats to validity likely to operate on the findings. For this reason, it is important to summarise any information provided by the researcher about the methods and data he or she used, and to follow up references to other materials relating to the research where more detail may be given. Of course, here too, there could be a gap between the information we feel we need and that provided.

Identifying the main arguments and evidence

The most central task in understanding an ethnographic study is to identify its main findings and the evidence presented in support of them.[8] I will deal with these separately.

Main claims

Above, I drew a distinction between research focus and case (or cases) studied. Corresponding to this, I will also make a distinction between the conclusions of a study (which relate to its focus) and the major claims (which relate to the case). So, in identifying the central claims of a study we are looking for those findings that refer specifically to the case(s) studied, leaving any that refer beyond this for later consideration as conclusions. Of course, there will often be considerable overlap in content between the major claims and the conclusions, that which is found in the case(s) studied perhaps being generalised to other cases. But the distinction between the two is important because assessing the validity of such generalisations is an added task over and above the assessment of the claims themselves.

Within any research report there will be a host of claims made, and the task of identifying the main ones involves detecting the structure of the overall argument. Usually this is not too difficult: authors will indicate to one degree or another which are the most important points they are making and how the others relate to them. We can also rely on our understanding of the focus and goal of the account, though it is always possible that we may find it necessary to revise this or to conclude that there are inconsistencies in the report between the stated goal and the actual argument.

In seeking to identify the main arguments in an ethnographic study, a useful starting point is, of course, any summary provided by the writer. Summaries may occur at the end of articles (or in concluding chapters of books) or they may come earlier. Here, for example, is the author's summary (provided quite near the beginning of the article) of Rist's account of the effects of variations in teachers' expectations on pupil performance in the kindergarten and early grades of an inner-city school in the United States:

The argument may be succinctly stated in five propositions.

First, the kindergarten teacher possessed a roughly constructed 'ideal type' as to what characteristics were necessary for any given student to achieve 'success' both in the public school and in the larger society. These characteristics appeared to be, in significant part, related to social class criteria.

Second, upon first meeting her students at the beginning of the school year, subjective evaluations were made of the students as to possession or absence of the desired traits necessary for anticipated 'success'. On the basis of the evaluation, the class was divided into groups expected to succeed (termed by the teacher 'fast learners') and those anticipated to fail (termed 'slow learners').

Third, differential treatment was accorded to the two groups in the classroom, with the group designated as 'fast learners' receiving the majority of the teaching time, reward-directed behavior, and attention from the teacher. Those designated as 'slow learners' were taught infrequently, subjected to more frequent control-oriented behavior, and received little if any supportive behavior from the teacher.

Fourth, the interactional patterns between the teacher and the various groups in her class became rigidified, taking on caste-like characteristics, during the course of the school year, with the gap in completion of academic material between the two groups widening as the school year progressed.

Fifth, a similar process occurred in later years of schooling, but the teachers no longer relied on subjectively interpreted data as the basis for ascertaining differences in students. Rather, they were able to utilize a variety of informational sources related to past performance as the basis for classroom grouping.

> (Rist 1970:413–4; paragraphs have been introduced
> into this extract for purposes of clarification.)

Such summaries are extremely useful in giving us a sense of what the overall argument of a study is. However, we should not rely on them entirely. Sometimes we will find that, in our judgement at least, they are not entirely accurate or complete. For example, in making my own summary of Rist's main claims I included one that he omitted: that the pupils themselves responded differentially to the teacher's behaviour towards them, in ways that reinforced the teacher's expectations. Also, where Rist refers to two groups of children in the summary (fast and slow learners) in fact the teachers he studied each divided their classes into three groups, though still ranging from 'fast' to 'slow'.

While summaries provided by the author are useful, then, they are no substitute for one's own careful reading of the whole text. At the very least, one may find differences in emphasis between the summary and the actual account, and sometimes there can be important discrepancies. It is also worth noting that authors may mix what I have distinguished as claims and conclusions.

To illustrate the sort of argumentative structure one is likely to find in ethnographic studies, here is an extended extract from a book reporting an investigation of juvenile courts. The extract deals primarily with one of the two courts studied (Countyside Court; City Court is the other one). As an exercise you might find it useful to note down what you take to be the main points, and the evidence offered in support, as you read the extract.[9]

ABUSING JUSTICE: THE IMPACT OF SOCIAL CLASS

It would be a naive argument that the social class differential between magistrates and defendants was in itself the key issue in the 'objectification' of the defendants and the creation of punitive justice. To say that magistrates are middle aged and middle class seems almost a truism since it is clearly observable and documented (Burney 1979). Most criminal defendants are from working-class backgrounds. In Countyside the gulf, the social distance between the bench and defendants, was considerable and clearly brought home by the frequency with which magistrates had to quit the bench abruptly for specific hearings because they knew defendants and their parents personally from acting as employer, head teacher, councillor and so on. The magistrates were, in the main, professional or propertied people and the defendants were, by and large, from one of the most deprived urban areas in the United Kingdom. It is obviously dangerous to generalize, but so often did defendants and parents have the appearance of being materially poor that we feel obliged to refer to this. Even more so than in City, we were left with the impression of poverty.

We can hypothesize, on the basis of our work in City courts, that the social distance between judge and judged, which was present there also, need not produce either the 'objectification' of defendants or harsh juvenile justice. We would argue that City's operational rules, part of the court culture, honoured the safeguards of due process and restricted sentencing discretion, thus preventing social class prejudices and antagonisms spilling over into court proceedings. Such safeguards appeared less real in Countyside. Further, Countyside clerks and magistrates tend to make 'space' in the court proceedings for restructuring by inserting extraneous ideological and 'common sense' agendas about how justice should be administered.

An ideal way of disguising this insertion of a hidden agenda vis-à-vis administering justice is to claim, as many magistrates did in conversation with us, that 'each case is judged on its merits'. The dynamics of this operation are complex but we will be arguing in this ... section that Countyside magistrates basically relied upon their own notions of adolescence, working-class family life, crime and its causes and the purpose of punishment. As a consequence of this, social class differentials, which as our analysis of City courts showed need not be influential, become so.

In this section we shall try to get over the obvious methodological difficulties of demonstrating the impact of social class on the administration of justice by using qualitative data taken from three sources. First, we had formal conversations with nearly all the magistrates who presided over observed sessions. That they happily met and talked with us, using the judgemental criteria we present below, is significant. Second, we draw on 'overheard' conversations between court officials, which took place during and after sessions, and between cases. Third, we draw on our own transcriptions of 'official' in-court discourse. We will deal with the impact of social distance by referring to issues of income, leisure and language.

First, we will consider Countyside officials' approach to matters relating to the income of poor people, the defendants and their parents. Fines in Countyside tend to be comparatively high and consistent with this was the magistrates' propensity to use compensation orders. In one case, which involved three boys convicted of stealing and joyriding a Daimler saloon, the juveniles were all sent to detention centre and banned from driving etc., but were also ordered to pay £200 compensation each. The compensation order was made in respect of repairs to the vehicle, although the court was aware that the bill had already been paid by the insurance company. One might wonder if the status of the car influenced this decision, not least because the presiding magistrates went out of their way to state, quite unsolicited, that the compensation had absolutely nothing at all to do with the car being a Daimler. Nor is it irrelevant to our analysis that when a juvenile sent to detention centre and ordered to pay £1,000 compensation (at £5 per week for four years) appealed to Crown Court against the sentence he had the compensation order quashed. It could be argued that sentencers, because of their cloistered social position, are unaware of the impact of demanding that an unemployed juvenile should pay over a third of his income for four years. There were occasions when this benign interpretation was given backing, in that magistrates would preface their sentence with suggestions of leniency:

We're just going to fine you £30 and £30 compensation.

Yet on occasions when parents offered to pay the whole sum of a fine there and then, rather than on weekly account, they clearly took court officials aback. On one occasion the clerk repeated the fine's amount slowly and said:

＿ You're sure you can pay this sum in whole now, today?

Thus, even the parent who responds to the formal sentence correctly, and without inviting social comment, receives it. Having so often and routinely quizzed defendants and parents about how much money they received each week, their hire purchase commitments, how much rent they paid and so on, court officials regarded relative affluence in a juvenile or his family almost as a form of defiance.

Countyside's officials displayed conservative attitudes towards leisure and the use of social space. Because they failed to consider leisure in the context of the lives of working-class adolescents, these attitudes proved judgemental and restrictive. Thus, in interrogating a boy as to what he does when not in school, a senior magistrate was told:

We play footie, go to the cinema if I've got money.

The reply from the bench was crisp:

Ah! You muck around all day and con your mother.

Adolescents are often reprimanded by magistrates for being on the street at all. Window-shopping is implicitly forbidden. Anyone window-shopping must be up to no good. One magistrate went as far as to suggest a kind of unofficial curfew for adolescents hanging around the village part of Countyside, with its proximity to the land of owner-occupied semi-detacheds:

It is a very serious thing to go wandering around the streets in Countyside village.

The use of complex language by court 'professionals' to 'cool out' defendants is well documented (Fears 1977). We do not intend to dwell on this device here, except to say it was, as one would expect, a routine feature of Countyside court.

So far we have dealt with specific examples of stigmatization, which appear to be a product of the social-class distance between judge and judged. The clearest evidence that the social distance structurally present between judgers and judged affects court procedures concerns Countyside officials' development of a full-blown thesis about the nature of poor families and their 'criminal' way of life. Our fieldwork diaries became so laden with 'problem family' explanations that we were forced to identify this as a working model amongst court officials in Countyside. This model is basically pathological, corresponding in part with those explanations of social problems found in the 'culture of poverty' thesis. The central strand concerns the belief that Countyside is infested by an underclass of criminal families. We were sometimes briefed during proceedings when a reputed member of the criminal families brigade appeared. On one occasion we were passed a note:

One of our regulars. They are one of our oldest customers ... his name is sprayed all over walls in the area.

These families, so the thesis goes, generally tend to be socially disordered. We note that clerks, perhaps unconsciously, confirmed this stereotyping in 'explaining' the sentencing decision to families, for instance by commenting in open court to a mother:

> I think one of your other sons is going to the attendance centre for a similar offence.

And to a boy disposed of with a fine:

> Perhaps, George, when your father comes out ... er ... comes out of prison, he'll help you pay.

Magistrates themselves expounded the criminal families thesis to us. One, for example, also a councillor, regarded them as nuisances and pollutants. He claimed to be pressurized by angry neighbours at his weekly surgeries, and favours a housing policy of moving them out, moving them on. In order to 'test' this thesis that there is a network of criminal families in Countyside, we analysed the names appearing on the juvenile court lists over the year during which we were observing. We found no evidence that such families existed as 'regular customers' of the juvenile court. When names did recur in the court, this was mainly the result of a series of remands. This might give an impression of recidivism but, certainly over the year's workload we analysed, there was no significant substantiation of the court officials' thesis. This particular ideological construction may stem from magistrates' other dealings with the local population as head teacher, councillor or employer. Whatever its source, it acts as a defence mechanism which can be utilized if the 'common-sense' principles court officials use in administering justice are ever challenged.

We have in this section relied heavily on extracts from official and unofficial discourse in and around the court to demonstrate our contention that the social-class position and subsequent cultural and ideological preferences of court officials spill over into the production of juvenile justice in Countyside court.

(Parker *et al.* 1981:87 92)

Here is my summary of the main claims in Parker *et al.*'s argument:

1. In Countyside Court there was 'objectification of offenders' and 'punitive justice' (pp. 87–8).
2. One possible reason for this was the sharp difference in the social class backgrounds of magistrates and defendants (p. 88).
3. But this, in itself, is not a sufficient explanation since a social class differential was present at City Court, and justice there was less harsh. The crucial factor was deviation from the safeguards of due process and restricted sentencing discretion which allowed magistrates to insert 'extraneous ideological

and "commonsense" agendas about how justice should be administered' (p. 88); agendas based on their own 'notions of adolescence, working class family life, crime and its causes and the purposes of punishment' (p. 88). These notions were a product of their social class background, as well as conservative in character and often inaccurate.

Summarising this account in terms of these three points obviously leaves a lot out, and some of this must be taken into account in any assessment of Parker *et al.*'s argument. Nonetheless, it seems to me that these are the main points made in this extract. Furthermore, they relate together in a coherent way, so that they can be read as forming a single overarching explanatory argument: justice in Countyside Court is relatively punitive because the effects of the social class differential between magistrates and defendants are not constrained by the operation of court procedures which elsewhere (such as at City Court) ensure due process and restrict sentencing discretion.

It will not always be possible to find a coherent overall argument like this. In book-length accounts, especially, one may sometimes find a set of main points that relate to one another in a looser manner, perhaps only in the sense that they all concern the same case. More usually, though, there will be some stronger form of organisation, often summarised as an argument in the conclusion or even presented in the introduction. Chapter titles may also provide clues to the overall argument, though they do not always do so.

It is worth noting that in identifying the main claims of an account one must be prepared to exercise some interpretative licence, since they may not be very clearly expressed. At the same time, though, it is necessary to ensure that the argument is not misrepresented. This is a matter of judgement; and sometimes different, but equally reasonable, versions of the main argument of a research report can be produced.

Evidential claims

Much of what is left out of the summary of Parker *et al.*'s argument that I provided above consists of the evidence they offer in support of their major claims. This is clearly important, and must be included in any summary of the extract that is to serve as a preliminary to its assessment. Here, then, is an account of the authors' argument that includes both the main claims and the evidence presented to support them.[10]

1. In Countyside Court there was 'objectification of offenders' and 'punitive justice' (p. 38).

    No evidence is presented directly in support of this claim in the extract, but some of the evidence used to establish the attitudes of magistrates might be interpreted as supporting it, such as the claim that fines tended to be high, the use of compensation orders (p. 39), and the public reprimands of defendants (p. 40).

2. One possible reason for the punitive treatment was the sharp difference in the social class backgrounds of magistrates and defendants (p. 38).

    The authors offer several arguments to support the claim that there was a social class differential between magistrates and defendants in Countyside Court:

    (a) published evidence and commonsense knowledge about the middle-class and middle-aged character of magistrates in general (p. 38).

    (b) the fact that at Countyside magistrates frequently 'had to quit the bench abruptly for specific hearings because they knew defendants and their parents personally from acting as employer, headteacher, councillor and so on' (p. 38).

    (c) the claims that 'The magistrates were, in the main, professional and propertied people', while 'The defendants were, by and large, from one of the most deprived urban areas in the United Kingdom' (p. 38).

    (d) the claim that often 'defendants and parents (had) the appearance of being materially poor' (p. 38).

3. The difference in social class backgrounds is not, in itself, a sufficient explanation since this is also found at City Court. Particularly important at Countyside were deviations from the safeguards of due process and restricted sentencing discretion which allowed magistrates there to act on the basis of class-based, conservative and inaccurate assumptions.

    A range of sorts of evidence is offered in support of this:

    (a) The authors report that: 'safeguards appear less real in Countyside' (p. 38).

    (b) Information (general and specific) is provided about Countyside officials' attitude towards the income levels of defendants and their parents (pp. 39–40):

    It is reported that fines tend to be comparatively high. (p. 39)

    Also, Countyside magistrates tend to use compensation orders:

(i)   A case is reported involving three boys: ordered to pay £200 compensation on top of a detention sentence and driving ban, even though repairs had already been paid for by the insurance company. The authors comment:

> One might wonder if the status of the car influenced this decision, not least because the presiding magistrates went out of their way to state, quite unsolicited, that the compensation had absolutely nothing at all to do with the car being a Daimler. (p. 39)

(ii)   Another case, this time of a juvenile sent to detention centre and ordered to pay £1000 compensation (at £5 per week for four years). He appealed to the Crown Court against the sentence and the compensation order was quashed. The authors point out that this compensation represented 'over a third of his income for four years' (p. 39).

(iii)   The authors offer what they call benign and less benign interpretations of these and other cases. The former is that the magistrates were unaware of the poverty of their defendants, hence the frequent comments by magistrates of the kind: 'we're *just* going to fine you £30 and £30 compensation' (p. 39). However, they also report contrary evidence which suggests the less benign interpretation that the magistrates intended the treatment to be harsh. They report that court officials showed shock when parents offered to pay fines in full. They comment on this:

> Thus, even the parent who responds to the formal sentence correctly and without inviting social comment receives it. Having so often routinely quizzed defendants and parents about how much money they received each week, their hire purchase commitments, how much rent they paid and so on, court officials regarded relative affluence in a juvenile or his family almost as a form of defiance. (p. 40)

(c)   The authors also report that 'Countyside's officials displayed conservative attitudes towards leisure and the use of social space' (p. 40):

(i)   A case is cited of a magistrate interrogating a boy about what he does when not in school, receiving the reply 'We play footie, go places, go to the cinema if I've got money', and commenting 'Ah! You muck around all day and con your mother' (p. 40).

(ii)   Adolescents were often reprimanded by magistrates for being on the street at all:

> Anyone window-shopping must be up to no good. One magistrate went as far as to suggest a kind of unofficial curfew for adolescents hanging around the village part of Countyside, with its proximity to the land of owner-occupied semi-detacheds: 'It is a very serious thing to go wandering around the streets in Countyside village'. (p. 40)

(d)   It is also claimed that court officials routinely used complex language to 'cool out' defendants. The only evidence relevant to this is a reference to another study: Fears (1977).

(e)   The authors report that 'The clearest evidence that the social distance structurally present between judgers and judged affects court procedure concerns Countyside officials' development of a full-blown thesis about the nature of poor families and their "criminal" way of life' (p. 40). They report that their fieldwork diaries became laden with ' "problem family" explanations' (p. 40). This criminal family thesis operated as a working model, and had as its central assumption that Countyside is infested by an underclass of criminal families which were viewed as socially disordered:

> On one occasion we were passed a note: 'One of our regulars. They are one of our oldest customers ... his name is sprayed all over walls in the area.' (p. 40)

Clerks confirmed this stereotyping in explaining sentencing to families:

> To a mother in open court: 'I think one of your other sons is going to the attendance centre for a similar offence.' (p. 41)

> To a boy given a fine: 'Perhaps, George, when your father comes out ... er ... comes out of prison, he'll help you pay.' (p. 41)

The criminal families thesis was also expounded in interviews with the researchers:

> One, (magistrate) ..., also a councillor, regarded them as nuisances and pollutants.' (p. 41)

Finally, the authors argue that the criminal families thesis is false:

> In order to 'test' this thesis that there is a network of criminal families in Countyside, we analysed the names appearing on the

juvenile court lists over the year during which we were observing. We found no evidence that such families existed as 'regular customers' of the juvenile court.' (p. 41)

This is not the only way in which Parker *et al.*'s evidence could be summarised, but I think it broadly captures the structure of their argument. In looking at the evidence listed here we should note that it is not all of a piece. Sometimes a claim stands on its own, sometimes it is supported by evidence, and sometimes that evidence is itself supported by further evidence. (I have tried to indicate something of this structure by indenting supporting arguments.)

Whether looking at main arguments or at evidence we must pay attention to the types of claim involved. In the next section I will look in more detail at these types.

Types of claim

There seem to me to be three kinds of argument typically found in ethnographic accounts (as main and/or as evidential claims). These can be listed under the following headings:[11]

1. Definitions,
2. Descriptions,
3. Explanations.

Definitions

Definitions tell us how a particular term is being used in an account. For instance, in introducing a distinction between teaching and survival strategies on the part of secondary school teachers, Woods provides the following definition of 'survival':

... It is, in short, a survival problem. What is at risk is not only (the teacher's) physical, mental and nervous safety and well-being, but also his continuance in professional life, his future prospects, his professional identity, his way of life, his status, his self-esteem ...

(Woods 1979a:145)

Woods is spelling out here what he means when he claims that teachers are concerned with survival. And he also defines 'teaching' (adopting the definition put forward by the philosopher Paul Hirst) as 'activity intended to bring about learning' (Hirst 1971).

It is very unlikely that the major claims of an ethnographic study would be definitional. However, definitions may well form part of the substructure of the argument. Also, while we would not expect to find evidence offered in support of definitions, reasons indicating their appropriateness may be provided.[12]

Descriptions

Descriptions are one of the most important sorts of argument to be found in ethnographic (and other kinds of) research reports, since explanations depend on them, and so do theories and evaluations. We cannot explain, generalise, theorise about, or evaluate something without describing it, or at least assuming some description of it.

What I mean by a description is a verbal or numerical representation of some feature of a scene. In the course of their account of justice at Countyside, Parker *et al.* present many descriptions. Indeed, one of their main claims in the extract quoted is a description: that Countyside justice is punitive.[13] What is being suggested here is that the same sorts of case receive more severe punishments at Countyside than they would elsewhere. The authors also provide descriptions as evidence. Thus, in seeking to illustrate the effects of the social class background of magistrates on Countyside justice, they describe court officials as displaying 'conservative attitudes towards leisure and the use of social space', and support this with further descriptive evidence in the form of two illustrative cases.

As I noted earlier, the naturalistic mode of writing tends to present descriptions as if they simply reproduced the phenomena described. Yet, they do not; they are always selective. We can always provide a very large number of (often mutually compatible) descriptions of the same scene. Descriptions represent phenomena from particular points of view that are designed to serve certain purposes, for example to provide evidence for other claims. So, in identifying descriptions, we need to pay attention to the function they are intended to serve and the relevances on which they are based. In large part this is a matter of noting how they fit into the argumentative structure of the account and how they relate to the research focus.

As an illustration of the selective character of descriptions, take the following brief description from Parker *et al.*: '(A clerk commented) in open court to a woman "I think one of your other sons is going to the attendance centre for a similar offence"' (Parker *et al.* 1981:91). We can see how not just the content of the utterance but also the fact that it was to the mother of the defendant, and that it was made in open court are relevant because the description is intended to illustrate the stereotyping of offenders and their families as belonging to a criminal underclass.

The implication is, I think, that such utterances not only reflect but also publicly reinforce court personnels' stereotypes. At the same time, though, it seems certain that there were many other features of that comment and its surrounding context which could have been mentioned, but which were judged irrelevant. For example, we are not told anything about the woman other than that she was a mother who had more than two sons, two being currently or recently defendants, at least one of whom was being sent to an attendance centre. We are told nothing about the clerk beyond the fact that he or she was a clerk. We are given the words spoken, but not told anything about tone of voice, facial expression, and so on, on the part of the clerk or about the woman's (or other people's) reactions to what was said. Nor do we know anything about what had happened before or what happened after this comment was made (other than that the court was in process). The information that could have been included in this description is virtually endless, and the same is true with all descriptions. Writers must select and include what they take to be relevant, and leave out the rest. As readers, though, we must bear in mind that this process of selection has occurred, since in assessing validity we may need to consider the reasonableness of the judgements about what was and was not treated as relevant (though, of course, this is always difficult without access to the original data).

There is another aspect of the selective character of descriptions that needs attention. We should note how a description like the one discussed above can itself be categorised in a variety of ways. The authors present the comment by the clerk as an instance of stereotyping on the part of court personnel, portraying the families of defendants as 'socially disordered'. However, we could treat it as many other things: as an example of talk in a relatively public setting, as an instance of male–female or of female–female talk (depending on the sex of the clerk), as (perhaps) an interchange between an older and a younger person, as an utterance indicating what was probably spurious uncertainty (it seems unlikely that the clerk was *actually* uncertain about the verdict on the other son), and so on. Here again, there is a wide range of possibilities; and the more detail there is in the original description, usually, the more alternative higher level descriptions are possible. As we shall see in Chapter 4, when it comes to assessing the validity of descriptions, we must bear in mind the possible relevance of both what has been left out of descriptions and of alternative interpretations of the evidence presented.

Another aspect of descriptions that must be given attention is the distinction between those dealing with singular events and generalisations. The description of a magistrate 'interrogating a boy about what he does when not in school' (p. 90) is about a single event. By contrast, the claim about Countyside court officials displaying conservative attitudes towards leisure is a generalisation about what many of them did on many occasions (it is a generalisation across magistrates and over time). And generalisations require additional evidence over and above what is required to support singular descriptions.

Explanations

Where descriptions provide an account of features of some phenomenon, explanations are concerned with why one or more of those features occurred, and seek to show that they are the product of particular factors (direct or indirect). Take Rist's study of teacher–pupil interaction in the early years of schooling. It is the central claim of his account that the differential school achievement of the children is in large part a product of the teachers' social class-based expectations of them. So in this study, besides providing descriptions of the teachers' procedures for allocating children to groups and of their interaction with members of these groups, Rist also makes an explanatory claim. Indeed, the descriptive claims are subordinated to the task of explanation; much as they are in the extract from Parker *et al.*, where the overall argument is concerned with explaining why justice at Countyside is relatively punitive.

Explanations may also operate in a subordinate role in ethnographic accounts. Thus, at one point in his study of medical students' experience of the clinical years of their course, Atkinson refers to the well-known phenomenon of ' "medical students' disease" – that is, the hypochondria to which medical students are prone' (Atkinson 1981a:21). He notes that this has been explained by others in terms of the stress and anxiety produced by extreme academic pressure, but he puts forward a different explanation: that it results from 'a heightened awareness of the clinical', indeed an 'absorption' in clinical matters:

Students became more or less adept at handling a complex symbolic domain in which disease categories and diagnostic inference figure pre-eminently. It should therefore come as little surprise that clinical understanding should come to occupy a dominant position in the students' repertoire of conceptual schemes.

(Atkinson 1981a:21–2)

What he is suggesting is that students' very familiarity with clinical interpretations leads them to apply these to things that others would interpret differently. This argument is not a major claim of Atkinson's study, but rather offers further support for his descriptive argument that in the clinical years of their course the students become 'absorbed, seduced almost, by the clinical gaze'. (p. 22)

It is in the nature of explanations that they rely on theoretical assumptions. Thus, Atkinson's explanation for medical students' hypochondria relies on the theoretical idea that when people are learning a new mode of interpretation there will be a tendency for them to 'over-use' it, applying it to circumstances that others would treat differently. If we did not find this assumption plausible, then we could not judge Atkinson's explanation persuasive (unless it were supported by some other plausible theoretical assumption). As we shall see, assessing the theoretical assumptions built into explanations is an important step in judging their validity. So, in identifying explanations, we need to look out for the theoretical assumptions that they presuppose.

Explanations, like descriptions, are also based on relevances.[14] For any phenomenon, we can identify a potentially infinite number of causes. There may be one or more immediate causes, and each of these can in turn be explained in terms of other causes, and so on, *ad infinitum*. Which (or which combination) of these a researcher selects will depend partly on how the explanation fits into the overall argument and its relation to the research focus. For instance, we may explain the differential performance of the children that Rist studied in terms of differences in academic ability or in their attitude to school. And each of these (along with Rist's own preferred explanatory factor, the teachers' expectations) could be explained on the basis of more remote factors, for example differences in the children's home background. Furthermore, the latter could, in turn, be explained by appeal to family histories, and/or to the nature of the local communities from which the children come. And these, again, may be accounted for on the basis of various features of the character and history of US society, notably its racial and class structure. And so on. The implication of this is that where explanations are presented we must look out for any indication of the relevances that have guided the selection of explanatory factors.

A note on value claims

Ethnographers sometimes put forward evaluations: they not only describe and explain phenomena but also express some view about them in terms of one or more values. Much ethnography explicitly shuns evaluative intent, being concerned with describing and explaining what *is* rather than what *ought to be*. However, ethnographic methods are increasingly being used in research that is labelled as evaluative (Fetterman 1984, Fetterman and Pitman 1986). Moreover, there is much scope for uncertainty and confusion here because very often ethnographic accounts set out to describe and explain phenomena in terms of relevances that relate to values. What is often not made clear is whether those values are simply being used to define the focus for factual investigation or whether the researcher is endorsing them and therefore engaging in evaluation (Foster *et al.* 1996). Here is an example of possible ambiguity, from a study of an industrial training unit for slow learners. The authors comment:

For the most part, it is not at all clear that the students' skills are significantly changed, in terms of their competence with industrial machinery. There is little or no sense of their progressing through graded tasks, and of measurable improvement in performance.

(Atkinson *et al.* 1981:255)

Here, the terms 'significantly' and 'improvement' suggest evaluation, but it may be that what is intended is no more than a description in terms of a framework of relevances that is premissed on value concerns, for example relating to the stated goals of the unit.

It is my view that research cannot provide the sole basis for value conclusions, and that researchers should avoid drawing such conclusions. This is, however, a controversial matter. So, it is important to note that if evaluative claims *are* being made, some justification for the values adopted may be required (to the extent that they are not the only reasonable ones or the only ones likely to be adopted by those concerned with the phenomena being evaluated).

Parker *et al.*'s book on juvenile courts is an example of an ethnographic study where the overall argument is explicitly value-based. In the first chapter, they present their research as an evaluation of two local juvenile courts in the Merseyside area. The evaluation is in terms of justice, an important element of this being the consistency of each court in its treatment of similar cases, and consistency between different courts. Following their account of Countyside Court which I quoted at some length earlier, they examine the Court's treatment of car offences and then conclude:

The punitive nature of the disposals vis-à-vis car offences is in itself important, but just as significant is the way in which this policy illustrates the inconsistency, and thus lack of rational sentencing policy, which is both created by, and reinforces, the administration of justice via class antagonism.

(Parker et al. 1981:92)

'Punitive' seems likely to be an evaluative as well as a descriptive term in this context, as also are 'inconsistency' and 'rational'. Furthermore, Parker *et al.* provide us with some information about the values underlying their evaluation in a concluding chapter, where they distinguish between natural and social justice – the latter involving consideration of the social conditions in which people live in deciding what is a just punishment.

Identifying conclusions

Earlier, I drew a distinction between major claims and conclusions, the former applying to the case, the latter going beyond it to deal with the focus of the study (where this is more general than the case). There are two ways in which this may be done: by drawing a theoretical conclusion (what I will call 'theoretical inference') or by generalising the findings in the case studied to a larger population of cases ('empirical generalisation').

Theoretical inference

As we saw, it is common for ethnographers to conceive of their goal as the production of theoretical descriptions. These are believed simultaneously to describe and explain the phenomena to which they refer, as well as accounting for other phenomena of the same type (and thereby offering a theory). In my view, such different tasks cannot be achieved by the same means; they place quite divergent requirements on the researcher (Hammersley 1992:ch. 1). Indeed, I believe that many of the weaknesses of ethnographic accounts stem from the failure to recognise this. By pursuing a composite set of goals, ethnographers often fail to achieve any of them very effectively. Probably the most important distinction to be made here is between a primary focus on the particular and a concern with the universal. Both descriptions and explanations refer to particular phenomena occurring in particular places at particular times. So too do empirical generalisations (though it will be many places and/or many times). Theories, on the other hand, are concerned with why one *type* of phenomenon tends to produce another (other things being equal) wherever instances of that type occur. (This universality is, of course, what gives theories their potential relevance to a wide audience.)

While studies concerned with theoretical claims do, of course, have an interest in particular phenomena, that interest is limited to the role that those phenomena can play in developing and testing the theory.

There are, however, some difficult questions about the nature of theory in the social sciences. As I noted in Chapter 1, a nineteenth century, positivist view of the nature of laws informed some early ethnographic work, both anthropological and sociological. From this point of view, laws identify regular, causal connexions between types of phenomena to be found wherever such phenomena occur, and these laws can be precisely formulated and their operation demonstrated. The model here was the laws of Newtonian physics. It was this conception of law that was used by defenders of case study method to deny claims that the statistical method represented the scientific study of the social world. It was argued that since that method could only produce probabilistic generalisations it did not generate laws and therefore was not scientific. This argument has been largely abandoned by ethnographers today, along with the commitment to the discovery of sociological laws. But little attention has been given by them to alternative conceptions of theory. This problem remains unresolved and all we can do for the moment is to bear the issue in mind when dealing with the theoretical claims that ethnographers make.[15]

It is rather rare to find ethnographic research explicitly and single-mindedly pursuing theoretical inference, the best examples still being Lindesmith's study of opiate addiction and Cressey's work on embezzlement (Lindesmith 1937 and 1968, Cressey 1950 and 1953). Much present-day ethnography is primarily concerned with description and explanation. However, broader theoretical claims are often made on the basis of these descriptions and explanations, and these should be noted (along with any indication of the basis on which the link between claims and theoretical conclusions is being made).

A fairly typical example of the sorts of theoretical claim made, and the kind of basis outlined for them, is provided by Woods in his study of subject choice processes in secondary schools. He argues that some schools in the English education system are more 'constrained' than others, and that the school he studied had an 'extra burden':

it was about to become a comprehensive, not uncontentiously in the area at large. This introduced extra problems of validation, for it was considered imperative by senior staff at the school that it be seen as 'working' by parents of erstwhile grammar school children. The traditional symbol of worthiness is examination results. A common device to 'improve' these is to present them in the form of percentages – that is, as proportions of those taking the examinations. ... Clearly, all this throws the utmost importance onto one's selection processes. And since most examination courses begin in the fourth year, it would appear that third year subject choice, wherein pupils 'choose' the courses they wish to pursue for the next two years, is of crucial importance.

(Woods 1979b:171–2)

What Woods is suggesting here is a theory that pressure on schools for 'good' examination results reduces the degree of choice that they give to pupils as regards fourth and fifth year courses. From this point of view Lowfield, the school he studied, might be regarded as a critical case because there (he claims) the theoretical variable (examination pressure) is at a high level compared to other schools. To the extent that this is true, we can draw some conclusions about the validity of the theory from information about what happened at Lowfield.

Empirical generalisation

Instead of using the ethnographic case study as a basis for theoretical conclusions, ethnographers may alternatively seek to generalise from it to an aggregate of cases that is of general interest. As I noted earlier, while relatively few people may be interested in what life was like in Winston Street, Washington D.C. in the 1960s, many more are probably interested in, say, the nature of black community life in the United States in the second half of the twentieth century. Thus, Hannerz effectively uses his study of a case that is of rather limited interest in itself as a basis for generalisation to a whole that is of much wider interest. And this is a very common strategy used by ethnographers.

However, ethnographers are often not very clear about the nature of the whole to which they are generalising. An example is Punch's (1979) study of policing in Amsterdam's *Warmeosstraat*. As we saw, he justifies his study of this case on the grounds that previous studies of the police have not taken account of the full range of conditions under which policing takes place, since there has been little investigation of police work in large 'cosmopolitan' city centres. Two questions arise from this. First, what population of metropolitan inner-cities is Punch seeking to generalise to on the basis of his research on the *Warmeosstraat*? Second, to the extent that this is intended to contribute to our knowledge of some larger picture of police practice, what are the boundaries of that picture?

Punch doeś not answer either of these questions very clearly, but presumably the answer to the latter (in broad terms) is that he is seeking to generalise about policing in Western societies in the late twentieth century.

Ethnographers are also often not clear about whether they are using theoretical inference or empirical generalisation to link their findings to their conclusions about the focus of the research. Frequently, there are appeals to both strategies without the difference between them being recognised. Punch's study illustrates this. While in some places he seems to be concerned with drawing empirical generalisations from his findings, elsewhere he appears to draw theoretical conclusions. Thus, in the final chapter of his book, he claims that:

> The relevance of this case study is that it sets out to examine the role that patrolmen play in the social life of the inner city with the intention of illuminating some of the micro-processes which contribute to a more general analysis of the nature and quality of social order in such an environment.
>
> (Punch 1979:179)

This could be interpreted as hinting at a theory about the social conditions that produce different types of social order and disorder.

Westley's study of *Violence and the Police* provides another example where both theoretical inference and empirical generalisation seem to be involved, but here it is possible to identify the two more clearly:

> The purpose of this study was not to describe the urban police departments of the United States but to articulate the ways in which the occupation and technology of policing gave rise to a set of shared human responses - in the form of attitudes and values. Insofar as we were successful in identifying some of the major components and problems of policing as an occupation and analyzing how these gave rise to police norms, the results should be applicable wherever these conditions hold. Obviously, they don't hold for all police departments. Some police departments were at that time so corrupt that there was almost no professional core to their activities, and 'our' department certainly did not represent them. Other departments were so highly professionalized and controlled by civil service regulations that most of the attitudes we described never developed. ... But between these two poles of high professionalization and widespread corruption we should guess that most of the major urban police departments in the United States would be found. We should argue that to the degree that any police department was faced with the conditions of public hostility, public pressure, political influence, and opportunities for graft, they would probably respond with

the normative system analogous to that described in this book. That many police departments held the same view of their work and of the public was at least partially demonstrated when a California newspaper posed our questions on secrecy to men from seven different departments in the San Francisco area and received almost identical responses.

(Westley 1970:xii)

Here, the primary basis for drawing conclusions seems to be theoretical inference. But the question of how far the conditions specified in the theory hold in various US police departments is also addressed.

In examining the conclusions drawn in ethnographic studies, then, we need to be attuned to whether theoretical inference or empirical generalisation, or both, are involved. In the case of theoretical conclusions we must be as clear as possible about the theory the case(s) have been used to develop and/or test and about why these are believed to provide the basis for theoretical inference. Where empirical generalisation is involved, we must look out for indications of the larger whole to which generalisation is being made, and for the reasons why such generalisation is believed to be sound.

Conclusion

In this chapter I have explored the task of understanding ethnographic accounts. I have emphasised that understanding texts is not a straightforward business: the meaning is not there on the page for us to pick up. We must work at making sense of what the author is telling us and why. And we should not take the author's own statements about the message as beyond revision. Authors are not always as clear and consistent as they might be and we must look at the claims they actually make, as well as those that they say they make.

I identified several aspects of ethnographic accounts that we should look out for: the focus, the case(s) studied, the methods used, the main claims and evidence, and, finally, any conclusions that are drawn.

Developing a summary account of an ethnographic text which covers these various elements provides us with a basis for the next step of our task: making an assessment of that account. But before we can do this, we must consider the question of the standards or criteria by which such assessment should be made. This is the task of the next chapter.

Notes

1. See, for example, Brown (1977), Atkinson (1982, 1990 and 1992), Edmondson (1984), Clifford (1983), Clifford and Marcus (1986), Marcus and Cushman (1982), Marcus and Fischer (1986), Geertz (1988), van Maanen (1988 and 1995).
2. I shall use these terms interchangeably. As might be expected, there is a close link between the commitment to naturalism on the part of ethnographers that I outlined in Chapter 1 and use of the naturalistic mode of presentation.
3. I found it in a school staffroom, see Hammersley (1980).
4. It is worth noting that experiments in ethnographic writing are not new. Bateson's *Naven* is a precursor to some of the more recent developments (Bateson 1958). Indeed, Jacobson argues that recent commentators have tended to neglect the degree of textual experimentation that went on in the past (Jacobson 1991). For an assessment of 'experimental' writing and the rationale for it, see Hammersley (1993a and 1995a:ch. 5).
5. I will look briefly at assessing the research process itself in Chapter 7.
6. This rationale illustrates the point I made in Chapter 1 about the balancing act that ethnographers often perform, maintaining distance both from science (or at least from quantitative research), and from literature.
7. See Spradley (1979) for discussion of the range of forms that ethnographic questions can take.
8. It is common to refer to the main claims of a study as its findings. I shall use this term on occasions myself, as here, but it is worth noting that it is potentially misleading. It may be taken to suggest that the researcher had little role in the research, that he or she merely *found* certain things to be the case. This usage matches the assumptions of ethnographic naturalism.
9. Since this is a relatively brief extract from one chapter of a book, its argument depends on material to be found elsewhere. Nevertheless, it will serve for the purposes of illustration.
10. In fact, the authors do not present evidence specifically in relation to the distinct components of their argument, but seek to support it as a whole. I have allocated the evidence to each of the claims as seems most appropriate. Also, note that I am not concerned here with the quality or validity of this evidence. I will look at this in Chapter 5.
11. These correspond broadly to the types of product mentioned in the earlier discussion of research focus, except for the inclusion of definitions (which rarely if ever constitute main claims) and the omission of theories (since these can only be conclusions, not claims about the case itself).
12. It is perhaps worth pointing out here that this book itself uses a number of terms in distinctive ways, notably 'focus', 'case', 'claim' and 'conclusion'. Definitions are provided but, as is always the case, there is a danger of confusion with other uses of these terms.
13. This claim is ambiguous: it may also be interpreted as an evaluation. For the moment I will deal with it as description.
14. For a useful discussion of this point, see Hart and Honoré (1985, Part I Section I, philosophical preliminaries).
15. For detailed discussions of the problem, see Hammersley (1989 and 1995b).

CHAPTER 3

Standards for assessing ethnographic research

The question of the standards by which ethnographic studies should be assessed is the point at which disagreements about the nature of ethnography are most sharply focused. It penetrates to the heart of the relationship between ethnography and quantitative research, and of that between both of these and the methods of natural science. Ethnographers are themselves divided on this issue. Some believe that the standards which are normally applied to quantitative research are also appropriate for qualitative research. Others argue for standards that are distinctive to ethnography. Yet others seem to reject the very issue of standards. I will look at each of these approaches, before outlining the approach that I will adopt.

There is by no means complete and clear agreement among quantitative researchers about the criteria in terms of which their research should be addressed. However, there are two sets of concepts that are commonly used to guide such assessment. The most comprehensive of these is the distinction between internal and external validity (Campbell 1957, Campbell and Stanley 1963, Cook and Campbell 1979). This distinction was developed in the context of experimental and quasi-experimental research, where the central concern is with hypothesis testing and how research can be designed so as to rule out various types of threat to validity. There is some ambiguity in the use of these terms, but (broadly speaking): 'internal validity' refers to whether (within a particular experiment) the treatment administered actually caused the predicted outcome; 'external validity' refers to whether this causal relationship can be generalised to other cases. There have been several attempts to apply this scheme to ethnographic research (Denzin 1978, Evans 1983, LeCompte and Goetz 1982, Goetz and LeCompte 1984).

My own view is that the basis of this distinction is unsound, since it assumes that the issue of whether a causal relationship has been discovered in the experimental situation is separate from the question of whether it occurs elsewhere. Yet, to claim that a causal relationship has been found in one case is necessarily to imply that a similar relationship will be found in other cases, even though we may not know in what types of cases. The very concept of cause implies a relationship that always (or probabilistically) occurs when certain conditions are met; and therefore it cannot refer to a single case alone. From this point of view, there is only one form of validity, not two. Campbell (1957) identifies a variety of types of threat to validity on the basis of the distinction between internal and external validity, and this discussion is of considerable value. However, the distinction itself is misleading (Hammersley 1991).

The other scheme in terms of which quantitative research is frequently assessed is framed by the concepts of reliability and validity. On most interpretations, this is less comprehensive than the distinction between internal and external validity, focusing primarily on measurement rather than the overall process of hypothesis testing. Generally speaking, 'validity' refers to accuracy of measurement, 'reliability' to consistency of measurement. There have also been several attempts to apply these concepts to ethnographic research (Denzin 1978, Evans 1983, Dobbert 1984, LeCompte and Goetz 1982, Goetz and LeCompte 1984, Kirk and Miller 1986).

Here again, though, there are conceptual problems. In large part these stem from the confusingly diverse ways in which the terms 'validity' and 'reliability' are used. There is divergence, for instance, about whether they refer to properties of measurement instruments, of observers, or of particular measurements; and about whether they are defined by the relationship between findings and the properties being measured, or by relationships among findings produced through using different measurement instruments (Hammersley 1987a). At the very least, some conceptual clarification is required. Furthermore, the restriction of the focus of this scheme to measurement means that, in its normal form, it is not sufficient in itself even for the assessment of quantitative studies.

In summary, then, while these quantitative concepts identify important considerations in the assessment of research, they do not provide an adequate conceptual basis for such assessment.

The argument that there are distinctive standards for judging ethnographic research usually draws on one or more of the three methodological assumptions (naturalism, understanding and discovery) that I outlined in Chapter 1. Thus, commitment to naturalism is often taken to imply that the sole assessment criterion should be whether the account accurately captures the phenomenon being described. This view can take at least two forms. The phenomenon may be defined as the perspectives of the people under study. Here the aim of ethnography is to map the perceptions and interpretations of participants, and perhaps also to document the cultural resources by which these were produced. More commonly, the phenomenon being described goes beyond participants' understandings and includes their behaviour and its wider context. On both interpretations, though, the appropriate criterion of assessment is the extent to which the people's perspectives and/or behaviour and context are accurately captured.

The influence of naturalism and of the other two assumptions can be seen in some of the distinctive standards that have been proposed for ethnographic research, but there are other influences too – notably, an emphasis on theory development. Here is a composite list of assessment criteria that have been recommended as distinctive to ethnography by a number of writers (Frake 1962, Lofland 1974, Wolcott 1975, Owens 1982, Miles and Huberman 1984, Athens 1984, Lincoln and Guba 1985):

1. The extent to which substantive and formal theory are produced and the degree of development of the theory;[1]
2. The novelty of the claims made;
3. The consistency of the claims with empirical observations;
4. The credibility of the account to readers and/or to those studied;
5. The degree to which the cultural description produced provides a basis for competent performance in the culture studied;
6. The extent to which the findings are transferable to other settings;
7. The reflexivity of the account: the degree to which the effects of research strategies on the findings are assessed and/or the amount of information about the research process that is provided to readers.

There is much to be learned from these criteria, but in my view they are not acceptable as they stand. For instance, the first applies only to research that is concerned with producing theory. It could not be a general standard of assessment, unless we were to insist that all ethnography be directed towards producing theory, and there seems no good reason to do so. Another problem is that several of these considerations (notably the third, fourth, fifth and seventh) refer to *means* of assessment rather than to a *standard* in terms of which assessment should be made.[2] Finally, it is questionable whether these criteria are specific to ethnography. In my view, to the extent that they capture important issues, they are equally applicable to quantitative research.

As I mentioned earlier, there are some qualitative researchers who question the need for standards of assessment. For example,

Smith (1989 and 1993) has argued that from the intepretivist or relativist position he adopts there are no abstract or general standards in terms of which the validity of claims to knowledge can be judged. We can do no more than describe the forms of justification used in particular epistemic communities at particular times. Thus, he argues that 'valid' is a label that is applied to an account with which one agrees. And the basis for agreement is that interpreters share similar values and interests (Smith and Heshusius 1986:8–9). He concludes that:

To accept that social reality is mind-constructed and that there are multiple realities, is to deny that there are any 'givens' upon which to found knowledge. If one accepts these assumptions, different claims about reality result not from incorrect procedures but may simply be a case of one investigator's interpretation of reality versus another's.

(Smith 1984:383)

At the same time, Smith suggests that considerations of a moral kind should inform the assessment of knowledge claims. Here he takes over the philosopher Richard Rorty's argument that inquiry should aim at promoting human solidarity (Smith 1993, Rorty 1991).

This position suffers from the usual problem with relativism, it involves a performative contradiction: to deny the existence of general standards is itself to make a general claim; and on what basis are we to judge the validity of this? It seems that while all other claims are to be treated as only true *relative to someone's point of view*, relativism demands that its own validity be accepted as *absolute*. Much of the force of Smith's argument lies in his emphasis on the unavailability of algorithmic criteria for assessing the validity of knowledge claims, criteria which provide absolute certainty. Yet, we can accept that judgements of validity are always fallible without adopting the relativistic position Smith proposes (Hammersley 1992:ch. 4).

Putting relativism on one side, the two approaches to the identification of standards of assessment that I have outlined differ primarily in terms of whether they treat ethnography as sharing broadly the same methodological framework as quantitative research or as based on quite different methodological assumptions. Adopting the first approach the task becomes that of applying (and perhaps modifying) the criteria used by quantitative researchers to the case of ethnography. The second approach has generally taken the form of seeking to identify the criteria actually used by ethnographers. But, as I have suggested, neither approach is satisfactory as it stands, and in part this stems from a failure to address the most important question that needs to be asked before we can decide on standards of assessment: what is research for, what function should it be designed to serve? In my view, put baldly, its function is to produce knowledge that is of public relevance. This goal applies as much to ethnography as to other sorts of social research. And so too do the twin standards of validity and relevance that can be derived from it. In discussing these standards I will fill in more detail about the view of social research on which they are based. And, as we shall see, straightforward as it may seem, this definition of the function of social research is not without difficulties or beyond dispute.

Validity

By 'validity' I mean truth: the extent to which an account accurately represents the phenomena to which it refers. As I noted in Chapter 1, there are some social scientists who deny that ethnography can have validity in this sense, arguing that it is unscientific. There are also some ethnographers who deny the applicability of the concept of truth to their work. They argue that any claim to represent the social world is false or inappropriate because no such representation can ever be possible. I will address both these arguments.

A common view of the process of assessment as it occurs in the natural sciences (and by extension of how it ought to operate in the social sciences) is what we might call the replication model. Here, fellow scientists read research reports and set about replicating the experiments described to discover whether the same results can be produced. If they can, the claims made by the original researchers are accepted into the body of scientific knowledge; if the results are not reproduced, then the original researcher's claims are rejected as spurious.

There are severe limits on the possibility and practice of replication in the social sciences, and especially in ethnography. This is not just because of ethical limitations concerning the use of experiments on human beings, but also because (even within experiments) people's behaviour cannot be controlled to the same degree as can that of inanimate objects or other animals. More than this, the attempt to control variables by means of experimental manipulation affects the behaviour of the people being studied, raising the question of whether it is possible to draw conclusions from experiments about what people would do in everyday life. This is often referred to as the problem of reactivity, and it is in an attempt to avoid this threat to validity that ethnographers study 'natural' situations and seek to minimise the effects of the research on them. The result of this is that replication is difficult, if not impossible, in ethnographic research. Restudies of the same setting are sometimes carried out, but they may focus on different aspects of the setting, and have to take account of changes that have occurred during the intervening period. Of course, it is possible in principle for readers to try to check the results of ethnographic enquiry by mounting their own research in the same setting as the original study (though usually settings are anonymous and therefore not identifiable), or in settings that are similar to the original one. However, the difficulties and costs of doing this are considerable, and the results are likely to be less than fully conclusive.

Even in the physical sciences relpication is not as straightforward as it is sometimes assumed to be, though. For example:

1. It is not always clear when replication of an experiment has or has not been achieved, or what it requires. Complete information about experimental procedure can never be provided, and it is not always clear what sorts of variation should and should not affect the outcome of the experiment (Collins 1975, see also Franklin 1994 and Collins 1994).
2. The results of a replication are not as easy to interpret as is sometimes implied. There are reasons why the claims may still be true even though the replication failed to produce the same results, and vice versa. This is because scientists rely on theoretical assumptions in interpreting the findings of the original study and of any replication. As a result, both are open to potentially conflicting interpretations.
3. Replication is not always possible in natural science, and even when it is possible it may not always be judged necessary. Michael Polanyi provides an example of this:

> A series of simple experiments were published in June 1947 in the Proceedings of the Royal Society by Lord Rayleigh – a distinguished Fellow of the Society – purporting to show that hydrogen atoms striking a metal wire transmit to it energies up to a hundred electron volts. This, if true, would have been far more revolutionary than the discovery of atomic fission by Otto Hahn. Yet, when I asked physicists what they thought about it, they only shrugged their shoulders. They could not find fault with the experiment yet not one believed in its results, nor thought it worthwhile to repeat it. They just ignored it. ... It appeared that the physicists missed nothing by disregarding these findings.
>
> (Polanyi 1968:4–5)

I would not want to deny that the assessment of claims in the natural sciences is often more conclusive than it is in the social sciences, and that replication makes some contribution to this. However, even in the natural sciences there is an ineradicable element of judgement and uncertainty involved in the process of assessing the products of research. Natural scientists do not operate on the basis of the mechanical formula: if replication reproduces the findings accept them, if it does not then reject them. Rather, they interpret the product and process of the original research and of any replications in terms of the plausibility of the findings, and the effects of likely sources of error, and then make a judgement about validity on this basis. Replication may be an important aid for them in making this judgement, but it cannot replace the judgement; and sometimes judgement is (or has to be) made without it. So, the argument that ethnographic studies are not scientific because they cannot easily be replicated is based on a false conception of the role of replication in natural science. Our inability to replicate ethnographic findings does not undermine assessments of their validity, though it may make the task more difficult.

Let me turn now to questioning of the criterion of validity from the other direction: on the grounds that the very idea that ethnographic accounts can represent social reality is false. There are at least two arguments used to support such doubts.

One is that the use of the term 'truth' implies the possession of knowledge that is absolutely certain (that is proven beyond all possible doubt), yet knowledge can never be certain in this sense. Critics point out that in deciding on the validity or otherwise of some claim we always rely on assumptions whose own validity we must presuppose. And if we seek to test any of those presuppositions, we will be forced to rely on further assumptions. For instance, even in simple measurements of physical objects with a ruler we make assumptions about the properties of rigid bodies (that is of both ruler and object), such as that small changes in temperature will not have any significant effect on our measurements. And testing those assumptions would require us to measure heat, for example, which itself involves assumptions about the operation of thermometers, and so on.

The second half of the above argument is sound; but the first (that use of the concept of truth implies knowledge that is certain beyond all possible doubt) is not. To claim that a statement is true is not incompatible with a recognition that it may be false. I believe that we can never be absolutely certain about the truth of anything, not even in the natural sciences or in our personal lives. On the other hand, there are many things about whose truth we are very confident and about which we have every right to be confident. What I am arguing here is that we can have good reasons for believing that something is true or false without ever being absolutely certain about the validity of the claim. We rely on a whole host of assumptions about the world in our everyday lives, and while many of them are probably approximately true we can never be absolutely sure of the truth of any of them. Yet this ever-present uncertainty does not undermine our use of the concept of truth in that context, and it should not do so in research either.

A second source of problems with 'truth' arises from beliefs about the distinctive character of human social life. There are those who hold that in the case of social phenomena there is no single reality to which ethnographic claims correspond or do not correspond. It is argued that it is characteristic of human beings that they create multiple social worlds or realities, that all perception and cognition involves the *construction* of phenomena rather than their mere discovery. From this point of view, it may be concluded that contradictory views of 'the same' phenomena by different cultural groups are equally 'true' in their own terms. This argument is developed in a sophisticated form by Peter Winch in his criticisms of Evans-Pritchard's famous account of witchcraft among the Azande of central Africa. Winch notes that while seeking to understand Zande beliefs and practices, Evans-Pritchard none-theless treats them as false and ineffective because of what he 'knows' about reality on the basis of Western science. Winch argues, however, that this 'knowledge' is founded on a conception of reality that is *presupposed* by science rather than one that is *justified* by it, just as the Zande conception of reality is pre-supposed by their beliefs and practices. In other words, there is no independent basis on which we can judge between these two conceptions. In these terms magic is as real for the Azande as the reality depicted by science (or at least some of it!) is for us; there is no ground for claiming that the latter is 'more real' (Winch 1964).[3]

Of course, if we apply this argument to social research itself, we might see the latter as creating its own world (or, given the dissensus among social scientists, its own worlds). As we noted earlier, an example of such anti-realism is to be found among those who have given attention to the character of ethnographic texts. Some have claimed that these texts do not represent phenomena that exist independently of them, but *create* the social worlds they purport to describe through textual strategies of various kinds. And these strategies are a reflection of Western culture. Effectively, the argument here is not just that we can never be sure of the truth or falsity of our claims about reality but that we have no grounds for believing that there is a single true account of any particular matter of fact. Rather, there can be contradictory truths, since all the knowledge we can ever have is formed by our culture, and that culture is only one of many.

While this argument makes an important point about the limits and difficulties placed on understanding by cultural diversity, the conclusion that there are no phenomena independent of the researcher for her or him to document does not follow from it. All social phenomena are human products and are therefore (in some senses) not independent of humanity as a whole. But much social life is independent of any particular researcher or group of researchers. Furthermore, we are able to learn other cultures to one degree or another, and thereby to understand human behaviour that is framed in terms of them. And this implies some commonalities among cultures on which knowledge may be built. It is also worth pointing out that to claim that there are other cultures besides one's own itself implies that there is an overarching world in which these multiple cultures are to be found. In this way, as noted earlier, anti-realism or relativism is self-contradictory: if it is true that all perceptions and cognitions are culturally determined then this idea that the world is multicultural is itself a figment of a particular cultural imagination.

These two anti-realist arguments about truth certainly count against 'naive realism': the idea that there is a single world independent of us about which we have direct (and therefore certain) knowledge. And to the extent that ethnography is wedded to such a view, as it sometimes seems to be under the influence of naturalism, these arguments are sound criticisms of it. However, in taking account of these arguments, we do not need to abandon the concept of truth as the correspondence of accounts to phenomena that are independent of them. We can retain this concept of truth by adopting a more subtle realism. I have already introduced the key elements of this point of view, but they can be summarised as follows:

- No knowledge is certain, but knowledge claims can be judged in terms of their likely truth.
- There are phenomena independent of us as researchers or readers of which we can have such knowledge.

In my view, then, there is no reason to abandon the concept of truth or validity as a standard for assessing research findings. Indeed, were we to do so it is difficult to see what justification there could be for research as an activity.

Of course, even if we accept that validity is a feasible and legitimate standard in terms of which to assess ethnographic research, the question remains: on what basis can that assessment be carried out, given that replication is so difficult and that there is no foundation of absolute knowledge by means of which ethnographers can validate their accounts? The only basis left, it seems to me, is our judgements of the likelihood of error. From this point of view, there are three steps in assessing the validity of ethnographic claims:

1. The first question that we must ask about a knowledge claim is how plausible it is; that is, whether or not it is very likely to be true given what we currently take to be well-established knowledge. In the case of some claims, they will be so plausible that we can reasonably accept them at face value, without needing to know anything about how the writer came to formulate them or what evidence there is to support them. However, this will rarely, if ever, be the case with the main findings of a piece of research. The first test, then, is plausibility.

2. A second question we may need to ask is whether it seems likely that the ethnographer's judgement of matters relating to the claim are accurate given the nature of the phenomena concerned, the circumstances of the research, the characteristics of the researcher, and so on. I will call this 'credibility'. As with plausibility, there are claims whose credibility is such that we can reasonably accept them without further ado, but this is rarely true of the main claims of a study.

3. Where we conclude that a claim is neither sufficiently plausible nor sufficiently credible, we will require evidence to be convinced of its validity. However, when we examine the evidence we shall have to employ much the same means to assess its validity as we applied to the claim itself: we will judge *its* plausibility and credibility. And, of course, we may require further evidence to support the evidence, which we will again judge in terms of plausibility and credibility.

In many respects, this seems to me to be the way we judge claims, our own and those of others, in everyday life. This is not done on a purely individual basis of course. As co-participants in various communal activities we compare our judgements with those of others; and where there are disagreements these may be resolved by discussion aimed at discovering the truth, though in practical life they may equally be resolved by means of negotiation, delegation, majority decision, or even the exercise of coercion. Needless to say, plausibility and credibility are a relatively weak basis for judging scientific claims, compared to the idea that we can assess them directly according to their correspondence with reality or by relying on some body of knowledge whose validity is certain. This approach provides no guarantee that our judgements will be correct, nor any way of knowing for certain whether they *are* correct. Nor will judgements necessarily be consensual, since there may be different views about what is plausible and credible. And the effect of treating the basis on which validity is assessed in science as similar to its assessment in everyday life is to de-emphasise the difference between the two.

We must accept the weakness of this basis, I think, but recognise that it is the only one we have, and that it does not exclude the possibility of cumulative knowledge. Nor does it imply that there should be *no* differences between everyday assessments of validity and those carried out in the natural and social sciences. The key difference, in my view, is that researchers *specialise* in inquiry, whereas in everyday life inquiry is a minor and subordinate element of other activities. And the other side of this is that the publication of research findings involves a claim to authority; and such publications are often accorded more authority than the judgements of non-researchers. We must ask, therefore, on what basis this authority can be founded. The justification seems to me to lie in a form of social organisation, especially characteristic of natural science, that subjects claims to a kind of validity checking that is more consistently stringent than that in most other spheres of life, and where there are sustained attempts to resolve disagreements by discussion and further inquiry, rather than by other means. From this point of view, the scientific community has three key norms:[4]

1. All findings are subjected to communal assessment of their validity in which there is an effort to resolve disagreements by seeking common ground and trying to work back to a resolution of the dispute by relying only on what is accepted as valid by all disputants. This rules out the dismissal of arguments on the basis of the personal and social character-istics of the person advancing them.
2. Researchers are willing to change their views if such arguments from common ground suggest those views are false; and they assume (and behave as if) fellow researchers have the same attitude.
3. The research community is open to participation by anyone able and willing to operate on the basis of the first two rules.

A research community operating according to these rules maxi-mises the chances of discovering error in assumptions about what is plausible and credible. It also maximises the possibility of rational consensus. In these ways it encourages the cumulative development of knowledge; and it is for this reason that scientific knowledge is more likely to be true than are commonsense views about the same issues. This is not to say that in any particular instance current scientific knowledge will be correct and commonsense wrong, simply that scientific knowledge is likely to be closer to the truth on the average. Furthermore, it should be noted that this advantage is bought at some cost in terms of the time taken to resolve inquiries in this way; indeed, there is a possibility that agreement will never be reached. This means that scientists have to leave many potential research problems on one side until further notice because they offer no prospect of being resolved in a way that is convincing within the research community.

Even natural science does not conform perfectly to this ideal of communal organisation; though it approximates to it more closely than does social science. In the natural sciences obstacles to the operation of the three rules are likely to come mainly from individuals' personal commitment to particular theories and facts on the basis of their career interests.[5] While other interests, such as religious and political commitments, play a role in some areas of natural science (such as the study of evolution and nuclear power), in general they have little influence. In the social sciences, on the other hand, such commitments have a much more wide-ranging influence because the topics investigated usually have much more direct social significance. Such commitments have the effect of reducing the likelihood that views will be changed on the basis of counter-argument; and that others will be seen as prepared to change *their* views. Nevertheless, it seems to me that to the extent that social scientists have an obligation to maximise the chances that their findings are valid, the aim should be to approximate to the process of assessment that this model implies. What this means is that in judging claims we must rely not just on our own assumptions about their plausibility and credibility, but also on what we take as likely to be the judgements of other members of the research community. Anything that we do not find plausible or credible, or that we believe a substantial number of others will not find plausible or credible, requires support from evidence that *is* so regarded. In other words, just as researchers must write with the anticipated assumptions of their audience in mind, providing evidence sufficient to convince that audience, so as readers we must judge claims not only in relation to our own assumptions but also in relation to those that we expect to be accepted as beyond reasonable doubt by other members of the research community.

Truth or validity is the first standard, then, in terms of which I believe that ethnographic accounts should be judged; and in the next chapter I will look in more detail at how this can be done. Before doing that, though, we must look at the second criterion, what I have called 'relevance'.

Relevance

In my view, to be of value research findings must not only be valid but also relevant to issues of actual or potential public concern; that is, to shared values. This second standard is rarely mentioned explicitly in discussions of criteria of assessment, whether those appealing to the quantitative tradition or those offering distinctive ethnographic criteria. One reason for this may be the influence on ethnographic thinking of what I have called naturalism and the naive realism associated with it. As I noted in Chapter 2, these ideas may lead us to believe that descriptions *reproduce* the phenomena to which they refer, thereby encouraging neglect of the multiple descriptions possible of any phenomenon. But it is important to recognise that reality is infinite in scope, and that any part of it can be described in a large number of ways. And, given this, ethnographers cannot take their task as being simply to describe the social world. They, and we as readers, must decide which facts are important and are therefore worth describing, and which are not.

So, our interest in facts (in everyday life as much as in social research) is selective. All descriptions are *for some purpose*, and the nature of the purpose will crucially shape the character of the description. If, say, we are describing a meeting, it will make a considerable difference whether our interest is in the political positions that are represented, the differential participation of men and women, variation in the form of public debate between this setting and similar situations in other cultures, or something else. The descriptions produced on the basis of these various interests may overlap, but equally they may be so different as to be not recognisably referring to the same meeting (though if we believe that they are all true they should not contradict one another). And there are any number of points of view from which we can describe a social phenomenon. So, too, with explanations. These will not only be concerned with accounting for some aspects of a phenomenon rather than others, but will also involve the selection of explanatory factors in terms of the purpose which the explanation is to serve, as well as on the basis of judgements about which factors have explanatory power.

It is also of significance in this context that ethnographic accounts are communications addressed to an audience. When we communicate with people they assume that we are telling them something that is likely to be of significance to them. If it turns out that we merely communicate facts, *any* facts, we will soon find that we have few listeners.[6] In the case of most social research the aim is to communicate with a relatively large audience (otherwise what would be the point of publication?); it follows from this that what is communicated should be relevant in some way to such an audience. The obvious questions that follow are: who are the appropriate audiences, and what sort of relevance should social research have for them?

As we saw in Chapter 1, one of the main criticisms of ethnography in recent times has come from those urging a closer relationship with practice. This amounts to the argument that practitioners (members of various occupations, interest groups, political parties and so on) should be the audience for research and that it should serve their purposes directly. This argument can be found both among those committed to an approach based on the model of the natural sciences and among those who reject this.

One version is what is often called the 'engineering' or 'applied science' model. Here particular pieces of research are to be judged in terms of whether (and how well) they resolve some problem faced by a group of practitioners. This view is typically associated with the idea that practical problems result from inadequate knowledge and can be resolved by the application of scientific method, with science perhaps eventually replacing ordinary practical knowledge. To date, this view has had relatively little impact on ethnography; though with the growing use of qualitative methods in applied research, often contracted by government departments that are under increasing pressure for accountability, greater influence is likely in the future. Perhaps more significantly, it is also the view that some practitioners take of the function of research, and is one of the bases on which research may be judged by them to be irrelevant to their needs.[7]

Somewhat more influential among ethnographers has been what I referred to in Chapter 1 as the emancipatory model. The main source here is Marxism. For Marx, as the famous quote has it, the point was not just to understand the world but to change it (Marx 1845). Thus, there is always pressure within Marxist scholarship for it to demonstrate its relevance to political practice; and some Marxists have conceptualised this link with practice in strong and direct terms. For example, Georg Lukacs believed that the work of Marxist intellectuals should be integral to the operation of the

Communist Party, conceived as the bearer of proletarian consciousness. He viewed this consciousness as an aspect of socio-historical process in which the Party comes to understand the world through transforming it.[8] There is little scope here for any independent role for intellectuals, but there are other approaches which allow somewhat more leeway, while retaining a strong link with practice, in principle at least. One is the 'critical theory' developed by the Frankfurt School of Marxism.

Critical research is designed to produce emancipation of oppressed groups through enlightenment, that is by enabling members of such groups to recognise their true interests. It is claimed that ideology prevents oppressed groups from understanding their situation and interests, and is therefore a major factor in sustaining their oppression. A central feature of the work of critical theorists is therefore ideology-critique. Critical research differs from conventional ethnography in at least two respects. First, the aim is not primarily to describe (or even to explain) the culture of the people studied but to identify the effects of ideology on that culture. Second, the instrumental success or otherwise of a critical theory in bringing about enlightenment and emancipation is a crucial, perhaps *the* crucial, aspect of any assessment of its validity. For example, Habermas (1987), whose early work has been very influential in this area, uses an analogy with psychoanalysis. The validity of psychoanalytic interpretations is partly judged by whether they are recognised as true by the patient and whether that recognition eliminates the symptoms; in other words they are judged by the success or otherwise of the therapeutic process, viewed as a self-reflective movement towards personal autonomy. Thus, critical research sets out to explain the nature of a social order in such a way that it serves as a catalyst for the transformation of that order.[9]

Similar ideas are to be found in some recent feminist writing about methodology. Many feminists define the goal of their research as the emancipation of women, rather than as the production of valid knowledge in itself (Mies 1983 and 1991, Harding 1987). Often combined with this is the claim that the truth can only be discovered in and through the struggle against women's oppression. And, as in the case of Habermas, this argument is sometimes taken one step further, suggesting that truth is to be judged in terms of contribution to the goal of emancipation. For example, '...the "truth" of a theory is not dependent on the application of certain methodological principles and rules, but on its potential to orient the processes of praxis towards progressive emancipation and humanization' (Mies

1983:124). Here validity as a criterion is itself redefined in terms of a strong interpretation of relevance.

In my view neither of these approaches advocating a very close relationship between research and practice is convincing. The applied science model adopts too narrow a conception of the contribution that research can make to practice, and allows this to be constrained by practitioners' perspectives. Much of the value of research, it seems to me, is that it addresses issues that are not of immediate concern to any particular set of practitioners, but which are nevertheless important. The most pressing problems are not always the most significant, nor can we assume that practitioners have a solid understanding of their problems or of their situations. We need not accept the rather monolithic conception of ideology adopted by critical researchers to recognise that people's under-standings of their world (and I am including researchers in this) are subject to biases and distortions of various kinds. We must not, therefore, treat practitioners' perspectives as automatically beyond reasonable doubt. Researchers must be free to question practitioner assumptions where this seems necessary.

By contrast, the emancipatory model suffers from too narrow a conception of the appropriate audience for research. It seems to be restricted to members of the group to be emancipated. This may be because, as in the case of most versions of feminism, the emancipation of this group has been adopted as the primary goal, and it is believed that emancipation must come from 'below' not 'above'. Presumably, from this point of view, other sorts of research, directed towards different goals and audiences, are legitimate (if less important). However, there is a version of the emancipatory model, most clearly exemplified in Marxism, in which the target oppressed group is effectively the only legitimate audience because only it has the capacity to emancipate all humanity. This is the historic mission assigned to the proletariat by Marx and Lukacs (Habermas is less clear on this point). But we must ask what reason there is to believe that the proletariat or any other group has such a historic mission (Hammersley 1992:ch. 6).

It is perhaps also worth noting that what is narrowly constrained in the emancipatory model is not just the audience but also the range of topics that are judged to be important. Only those directly related to the task of emancipation (however conceived) are relevant. This is a problem that extends beyond this model. The discipline of sociology has built into it a set of assumptions about what are important research topics. Sociology began in the nine-teenth century with an interest in the effects of socioeconomic change on society, viewed from the point of view of the twin values of equality and social order; and the issues that arose in that context (inequalities of reward and opportunity, class conflict, urbanisation, bureaucratisation, democratisation, the apparent loss of community and so on) remain at its centre. Other topics have been added, for example those arising from the discipline's role in the education of new professional groups: social workers, teachers, medical professionals and so on. The result is a rather hotchpotch pattern of concerns in terms of which topics are judged to be important or unimportant. This is something that has been highlighted by feminist critiques, which have pointed to the male-oriented character of many of the central issues dealt with by social research, and the neglect or low status given to topics that are often of greater importance to women: the lives of working women, personal relationships, child-bearing, the care of young children, family life and so on. This underlines the point that we must take care not to adopt an overly restrictive conception of what are relevant topics for research, especially where these rely on conventional views that do not stand up to close scrutiny.

Perhaps even more important than these points, however, is that both the applied science and emancipatory models misconceive the nature of practice, and effectively overestimate the contribution that research can make to it. Commonly associated with the applied science model, as the name implies, is the idea that practice can take the form of the *application* of scientific knowledge. What is involved here, it is assumed, is the implementation of rules or prescriptions. However, this is not a plausible conception of the nature of practice, as a variety of writers have argued (Schwab 1978, Lindblom and Cohen 1979, Schön 1987, Larmore 1987, Carr 1987). They have pointed out that it involves making decisions in light of multiple, schematic (and possibly conflicting) values that have to be interpreted in relation to concrete and changing situations about which we have limited information. It is not so much the pursuit of some fixed end state, but rather the preservation or improvement of a situation in the light of a set of values whose validity one accepts for the moment (while recognising that these values may need to be revised subsequently). Furthermore, in the course of such action we must take account of the likely consequences for other values and interests of any strategies and tactics employed. What I am emphasising here is the inevitably contextual character of practice, not just of judgement about what would be effective means but even of assessments of appropriate and reasonable goals.

While Habermas criticises the view of practice implied by the applied science model (Habermas 1973), in effect much critical research adopts a similarly ambitious conception of the relationship between theory and practice. Here the goal of practice is conceived as being to bring reality into line with theory. This is a view that derives from Marx and Hegel, both of whom regarded practice as taking place within a historical process conceived as leading (potentially at least) to the self-realisation of humanity, to an era of human freedom in which people's lives would exemplify the ideals that previously had been striven for but had been unachievable. In these terms, the view of practice I sketched above is treated as an accurate portrayal of life before emancipation, but not of human life as it ought to be and as it will be. However, in my judgement this perspective is utopian. There are no good reasons for supposing that the character of practice can be completely transformed in the manner claimed. Nor is it clear that this would be desirable.

Besides misconstruing the character of practice, these advocates of a close relationship between research and practice also overestimate the capacity of research to produce information that is needed by practitioners. Both seem to assume that whatever knowledge is required can be produced, and in a relatively straightforward way. While I would not want to declare any knowledge unobtainable in principle, I think it is clear that sometimes the knowledge that we would like is not easily accessible. After all, we have long wished to know more about cancer so as to prevent and cure it, and very considerable resources have been expended in pursuit of that knowledge. But while we now know a lot more than we did, we still lack some of the knowledge that we need. What this highlights is that producing the knowledge which is required may take a long time and require more resources than are available. Furthermore, and this is a very important point, it may well involve a complex division of labour among researchers, the result of which will be that many of the studies carried out will have only indirect relevance to the original problem. This recognition of the importance of a division of labour among researchers also implies that fellow researchers will often be the primary audience for research reports, even though the eventual outcome of the research process should be relevant for practitioners.

I have argued, then, that to be of value research findings must have public relevance, but that this must not be interpreted as implying that every research project, and even less every research report, must make a direct contribution of knowledge required by some narrowly defined group of practitioners. Rather, researchers must be allowed to address issues that are not of immediate concern to practitioners but which there are reasonable grounds for believing are of relevance to their practice, to address a wide variety of practitioner audiences, and to operate a division of labour so that researchers themselves will often serve as the primary audience for many research reports. Furthermore, the limitations on the capacity of research to contribute to practice must be recognised, limitations that arise from the nature of both practice and research (see Hammersley 1995a:ch. 7).

Conclusion

In this chapter I have looked at the issue of the standards by which ethnographic studies should be assessed. I argued that neither those approaches that seek to apply the criteria used in quantitative research nor those advocating distinctive ethnographic standards are satisfactory as they stand, though both capture important aspects of the process of assessment. I put forward two standards for the assessment of any social research: validity and relevance. I tried to show that the arguments that have been used to question the appropriateness of applying the criterion of validity to ethnography are not convincing, and that it is a reasonable standard of assessment. I also outlined something of the process by means of which validity could be assessed. In discussing the criterion of relevance, I sought to establish its importance and to clarify how it should be interpreted. In the following chapters I will look in more detail at the use of these two standards in the assessment of ethnographic research.

Notes

1. The distinction between substantive and formal theory comes from Glaser and Strauss (1967). Substantive theory deals with particular empirical areas like patient care, race relations, delinquency and so on. Formal theory is concerned with more abstract areas of sociological inquiry, such as stigma, deviant behaviour, authority and power.
2. This is analogous to some quantitative methodologists' attempts to define validity and reliability in terms of the results of the measurement process, rather than in terms of a relationship between measurements and what it was intended to measure. The classic case of this is the definition of intelligence as 'what intelligence tests measure'. In this chapter I am concerned with standards of assessment rather than with the means by which we assess studies in terms of those standards. I will address the latter issue in Chapter 4.
3. For a development of this argument into a 'critique of scientific reason', see Feyerabend (1975 and 1978).

4. This account of the norms of science is closely related to that of Merton (1973:chs 12 and 13).
5. The increasing commercialisation of research in higher education institutions, and elsewhere, involves additional threats, however. For instance, increased secrecy (because sales depend on confidence in products that could be undermined by public debate) threatens the very basis of the scientific community as I have defined it.
6. Of course, we do not merely communicate facts in everyday life; there are other kinds of discursive act, like questions, requests, commands and promises. But I am assuming that this is the primary form of discourse in social research. On the assumption of relevance in conversation, see Sperber and Wilson (1986).
7. For an argument along these lines in the context of educational research, and a response to it, see Hargreaves (1996) and Hammersley (1997).
8. On Lukacs, see Lichtheim (1970), Kolakowski (1978) and Jay (1984).
9. An example of an ethnographic study strongly influenced by the emancipatory model is Willis (1977).

CHAPTER 4

Making an assessment: validity

In discussing the criterion of validity in the previous chapter, I advocated a position which I called 'subtle realism'. While retaining the idea that true knowledge corresponds in relevant respects to the phenomena that we seek to represent, this view recognises that we can never be absolutely certain about the validity of any knowledge claim; but it suggests that we can still make reasonable judgements about the likely validity of such claims. I also outlined what I took to be the implications of this position for judging the validity of ethnographic findings: that it involves assessing their plausibility and credibility, and that of any evidence provided in support of them. Here I want to discuss this process of assessment in more detail, looking first at the examination of major claims and the evidence associated with them, and then at the assessment of conclusions about the research focus that are drawn on the basis of those claims.

Assessing major claims and evidence

In making an assessment of an ethnographic study we must consider each of its major and subordinate knowledge claims. One question here is how plausible the claims are on the basis of our existing knowledge. Let us say that we are faced with the following two claims, from Strong's study of paediatric consultations in Britain and the United States:

1. There was variation in whether both parents attended the consultation, and where only one attended it was usually the mother.
2. Where the father alone accompanied the child he was treated as a loving but incompetent substitute for the mother.

The first of these two claims seems to me to be very plausible, on the basis of what I (and I assume we all) know about British and American society, including experience of doctors' waiting rooms. I do not need any evidence or even any information about how the researcher came to this conclusion in order to accept its validity. And I suspect that others would not need evidence to be convinced either. In the case of the second claim, however, I cannot simply accept it. It is not that I find it *implausible*, but rather that it is not *so* plausible that it can be accepted at face value.

Few, if any, of the major claims in ethnographic studies are likely to be so plausible that they need no support; if they *were* they would not be news. Faced with a claim that is not sufficiently plausible to be accepted, the second step is to assess its credibility (as I defined this term in Chapter 3). Here the task is to decide whether the claim is of such a kind that an ethnographer, given what is known of the circumstances of the research, could have made a judgement about the validity of this claim with a very low chance of error. Here, of course, we must use what knowledge we have, or what we can reasonably infer, about how the research was carried out. For instance, we must look at whether the research involved the ethnographer's own observations or reliance on the accounts of informants, or both; what role the ethnographer adopted in the field, and so on. What must be estimated here are both the likelihood of error given the nature of the phenomenon and the chances of error arising from the character of the ethnographer's or informant's access to it and/or because of bias on their part.

As an illustration of such judgements about credibility, let us consider the research of Ray Rist into the effects of teachers' expectations on pupils' school performance (Rist 1970). In the course of his study, Rist makes claims about which pupils were put into which classroom groups by the kindergarten teacher he studied. In my view we can conclude that his judgement of this distribution is unlikely to be wrong, given that it involves a relatively simple matter of observation, that he observed the class regularly over a relatively long period, and that on this issue he seems unlikely to have been affected by bias. However, Rist also makes the claim that the three groups of children received differential treatment by the teacher. In my view, we should not accept this simply on the basis of his presence as observer in the situation. This is because multiple and uncertain judgements are involved, in the form of observations about amounts and types of attention given to pupils by the teacher over a lengthy period of time. Thus, while we might reasonably accept Rist's first claim as credible on the basis of what we know about his research, I do not believe that we should accept his second claim on the same basis.

If we find a claim very plausible or highly credible, then we should be prepared to accept it without evidence. However, if we judge a claim to be neither sufficiently plausible nor credible, then we must look to see whether the author has provided any evidence to support it. If not, then our conclusion must be that judgement should be suspended. If evidence *is* provided we must assess the validity of that evidence. And where that evidence is itself supported by further evidence, we may need to assess the latter too. As we saw in Chapter 2, claims can be of several types, and different sorts of evidence are appropriate to each. Below, I will look at each type of claim and the evidence required to support it.

Definitions

Definitions are not empirical claims about the world but statements about how the author is going to use a term, about what meaning is to be associated with it. As noted earlier, they are not likely to form part of the central claims of ethnographic studies. However, they may be an important element in the evidence required for such claims. And while they are not open to assessment in the same manner as factual claims, this does not mean that they are open to no assessment at all.

One obvious assessment we can make of a definition is whether it has sufficient clarity for the purposes being pursued. Where there is a standard usage of a term that is clear enough for the purposes at hand, no definition may be required. However, many social science concepts are ambiguous or uncertain in meaning, and yet are often used without definition. A notorious example is 'social class', which can have very different definitions, based on discrepant theoretical assumptions (for example those of Marx and Weber); though usage often relies on vaguer and less coherent assumptions. And many other concepts raise similar problems.

One that is quite frequently employed in ethnographic research today is 'subculture' (see Gelder and Thornton 1997). This term seems to have been introduced into US sociology in the late 1940s to refer to:

a sub-division of national culture, composed of a combination of factor-able social situations such as class status, ethnic background, regional and rural or urban residence, religious affiliation, but forming in their combination a functioning unity which has an integrated impact on the participating individual.

(Gordon 1947:40)

In the 1960s and 1970s, 'subculture' became widely used: in claiming that different social classes had distinctive lifestyles, beliefs and values; and in explanations for crime and delinquency. Both these applications involved a shift from Gordon's definition.

The first made one factor (social class) central, rather than interpreting the subculture as a product of the integrated effects of multiple factors. Similarly, usage of the term in the study of delinquency and crime diverged from its original definition in identifying delinquent subcultures primarily in terms of a commitment to one or another kind of deviant or criminal activity.

Another variation in interpretation is that whereas Gordon identified subcultures according to an observer's judgement about 'functioning unity', in much subsequent usage of the term a key element has been participants' recognition of belonging to a distinctive group. Indeed, 'subculture' is sometimes used effectively as a technical synonym for 'group'. Such a usage raises problems like: do different groups with similar lifestyles belong to the same subculture, or are they merely similar subcultures? And, if the former, how similar must they be to belong to the same subculture? Equally, we might ask how much change in beliefs, attitudes and behaviour is allowed before we must conclude that one subculture has died and another been born (or that a group has changed from one subculture to another)? Also, can a single person be a member of more than one subculture at the same time, or is membership of any subculture all-encompassing? And, as if this were not enough, it is worth pointing out that Gordon's original definition is by no means unproblematic. He describes subcultures as subdivisions of national cultures; but the term culture is itself ambiguous, sometimes being almost identical in meaning to 'society' (which seems to be the way Gordon uses the term), sometimes referring to beliefs and values rather than to actions and structures (and therefore being part of, or related to, rather than isomorphic with society). This ambiguity is inherited by 'subculture'. While the term 'subculture' is widely used, these conceptual issues are rarely addressed, and sometimes vagueness and uncertainty cause problems.[1] Nor are 'social class' and 'subculture' unusual in this respect. What has been said about them is true of other concepts that are routinely used in ethnographic studies.

Faced with uncertainty about the meaning of key concepts (whether or not definitions are provided) we must give attention to two aspects of that meaning: intension (the concept's relationship to other concepts) and extension (its relationship to instances).

To clarify intension requires identifying other elements of the network to which the concept belongs. Concepts get some of their meaning by forming part of a set of distinctions that is hierarchically organised. I can illustrate this by looking again at Woods' contrast between teaching and survival strategies on the part of secondary school teachers (see Chapter 2, Woods 1979a:ch. 7). We can note that, despite their differences, these are subtypes of a higher level category: teacher strategies. This opens up the question of what other types of classroom action teachers engage in besides strategies. Similarly, at the other end of this conceptual network, Woods himself identifies a variety of different sorts of survival strategy. Putting these two points together, we can see how the distinction between teaching and survival strategies forms part of a larger conceptual structure which can be represented diagrammatically (see Figure 1).

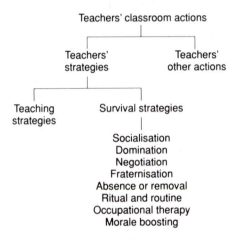

Figure 1   Woods' model of teachers' strategies

By mapping out conceptual networks of this kind we may be able to see weaknesses in the formulation of key terms. In the case of Woods' study, it seems to me that the distinction between strategies and other forms of classroom action on the part of teachers stands out as requiring clarification.

The second aspect of meaning, extension, concerns what instances would and would not count as instances of each category. Sometimes the problem of identifying instances may be quite difficult. Staying with the example from Woods, he argues that survival strategies:

...expand into teaching and around it, like some parasitic plant, and eventually in some cases the host might be completely killed off. However, like parasites, if they kill off the host, they are a failure and they must die too, for they stand starkly revealed for what they are. The best strategies are those that allow a modicum of education to seep through. Alternatively, they will appear as teaching, their survival value having a higher premium than their educational value.

(Woods 1979a:146–7)

While the definition of survival is reasonably clear in its intension, its extension is problematic: given that the concern with survival may masquerade as teaching, and that survival strategies may have educational value, how are we to distinguish instances of the two? This is not a problem that Woods addresses, but in my judgement it is of considerable importance if we are to assess the validity of his claims.[2]

Another basis on which we may criticise concepts used by ethnographers, and definitions of them, is that they fail to make distinctions that we believe are important, given the goal of the research. An example arises in Jean Anyon's report of a study of teacher–pupil relations in five elementary schools in the United States that cater for pupils from catchment areas differing sharply in social class composition. In discussing her findings she provides the following discussion:

A dominant theme that emerged in these two schools was student resistance. Although some amount of resistance appeared in every school in this study, in the working-class schools it was a dominant characteristic of student–teacher interaction. In the fifth grades there was both active and passive resistance to teachers' attempts to impose the curriculum. Active sabotage sometimes took place: someone put a bug in one student's desk; boys fell out of their chairs; they misplaced books; or forgot them; they engaged in minor theft from each other; sometimes they rudely interrupted the teacher. When I asked the children during interviews why they did these things they said, 'To get the teacher mad'; 'Because he don't teach us nothin''; 'They give us too many punishments'. When I asked them what the teachers should do, they said, 'Teach us some more'; 'Take us alone and help us'; 'Help us learn'.

The children also engaged in a good deal of resistance that was more passive. They often resisted by witholding their enthusiasm or attention on occasions when the teacher attempted to do something special. ... Passive resistance can also be seen on some occasions when the children do not respond to the teacher's questions. For example, they sit just staring at the board or the teacher while the teacher tries to get them to say the answer, any answer. On one such occasion, the teacher shouted sarcastically across the room to me, 'Just look at the motivation on their faces'. On occasions when teachers finally explode with impatience because nobody 'knows' the answer, one can see fleeting smiles flicker across some of the students' faces: they are pleased to see the teacher get angry, upset.

(Anyon 1981:11 12)

It has been argued, with some justification I think, that the concept of resistance used by Anyon here is insufficiently discriminating. As Hargreaves comments:

the mistake Anyon makes is to assume that acts of overt social protest are of the same nature as more minor transgressions, pranks and absences of enthusiasm.... Almost all pupil actions that fall short of absolute and willing compliance to teachers' demands are counted as resistance by her.
(Hargreaves 1984:31–2)

He contrasts this usage with the more restricted one found among other writers on pupils' orientation to school. They often distinguish a wide range of pupil adaptations, and recognise that not all of pupils' actions in the classroom are oriented primarily towards the teacher (Furlong 1976, Woods 1979a, Hammersley and Turner 1980).

Definitions may be an important part of ethnographic accounts, then; and even where they are absent they may need to be reconstructed (as far as this is possible). While they cannot be judged in empirical terms, we can assess their clarity and whether they make what seem to be the necessary distinctions given the purposes of the research.

Descriptions

Descriptions are accounts of the features of some set of phenomena (one or more) that exists (or has existed) in a particular place and time. The phenomena studied may vary in number and size (geographically and/or temporally). For example, at one extreme we could study the first five seconds of a telephone call (Schegloff 1968); at the other, we may investigate the labour process in contemporary societies and its development over time (Burawoy 1985). Most ethnographic research deals with phenomena that lie between these extremes in scope. But such variation is of considerable relevance to the assessment of evidence. This is because (other things being equal) the larger the phenomenon described, the more work is required to validate a description of it; since it is likely to involve multiple judgements and probably generalisation (from part to whole) as well.

Descriptions of small-scale phenomena

Let us begin with the simpler case, with descriptions of single and relatively small phenomena. There are two main considerations we must bear in mind in looking at evidence for such descriptions. First, how plausible and/or credible are the evidential claims themselves? Second, how convincing is the relationship between them and the claim they have been presented to support.

Validity of evidential claims Assessment of the validity of evidence must proceed in much the same fashion as I recommended in assessing the validity of major claims. To start with, we must assess their plausibility in terms of our existing knowledge. If they are very plausible, then we may simply accept them at face value. If not, we must assess their credibility.

In assessing credibility, we must take account of the process by which the evidential claims have been produced. The two most substantial sorts of evidence to be found in ethnographic studies are extracts from observational reports by the ethnographer and extracts from informants' accounts.[3]

The ethnographer's own observations will often be presented as extracts from fieldnotes or from transcriptions of audio- or video-recordings. An example in the extract from Parker *et al.*'s research on juvenile courts is the report of an offender who had been fined being told that, 'Perhaps, George, when your father comes out ... er ... comes out of prison, he'll help you pay' (1981:91). Such observations in court are presumably extracts from fieldnotes taken at the time.[4]

There are three general sources of error in observational reports that we need to consider. First, we must think about the potential effect of the research process and the characteristics of the researcher on the behaviour observed. This is the problem of *reactivity*.

In the case of Parker *et al.*'s research, I think we are reasonably safe in concluding that the researchers will have had little impact on court process, though we cannot be sure. The public nature of the events, the other constraints likely to be operating on the people involved, and the likelihood that the researchers were viewed as relatively low status, all point in this direction. However, reactivity is a problem that arises quite commonly in ethnographic research. An interesting example is provided by Pinch and Clark's study of market traders (Pinch and Clark 1986). This research involved video-recording the sales 'spiel' of the traders, and the latter sometimes used references in their sales talk to the research-ers' camera as representing a local TV company. The researchers also acted as 'ricks' or front men/women for the traders. As Cherrington *et al.* (1987) point out in a commentary on this article, it is possible that the research process may have exaggerated certain features of the behaviour of the traders in a way that threatens the validity of the findings. Of course, this problem of the research process itself affecting what is observed (what I will call the problem of *procedural reactivity*) does not arise where the research is covert (so long as the researcher's cover is not blown).

But it is always a potential problem when the people studied know they are being researched.

Equally important are the possible effects of the personal and social characteristics of the researcher on the behaviour observed; and these arise in both overt and covert research. Thus such factors as the age, gender, social class and professional identity of the researcher (or participants' perceptions of these) may affect what people do and say when being observed. The importance of the gender of the researcher has been emphasised by feminists and others, and there is no doubt that this factor can shape research findings significantly (Warren 1988). Age can also be important. Honigmann (1970:62) notes how his age alienated him 'from the younger men and women, especially those deviant from the larger society's norms', in his study of an Inuit community on Baffin Island. I will refer to this as personal reactivity.

Clearly, both procedural and personal reactivity can be a significant source of error in ethnographers' observations. However it is important to remember what is at issue here. It is not whether the research process or the characteristics of the researcher have affected the behaviour that was observed, but rather whether they have affected it in respects that are relevant to the claims made (and to a significant degree). Often, reactive effects may be judged likely to have occurred, but unlikely to have had a significant effect on the validity of the findings.

A second source of error, as I indicated in discussing the credibility of major claims, can arise from the nature of the feature being observed. Some features (such as which pupils are allocated to which classroom group) are less likely to be misperceived than others (such as the similarities or differences in the treatment of those groups). This is not a matter of some features being directly observed in a way that guarantees the validity of observational reports, while other features are merely inferred. All observations involve inference in a sense, but we can reasonably judge some inferences to be much more open to error than others.

Third, and equally important, we must consider the features of the researcher and of the circumstances in which the research was carried out; in so far as these might affect the validity of the ethnographer's reports. We need to think about the sorts of constraints under which observation occurred and the resulting danger of misperceiving what took place (especially when also trying to record it). Also, we must remember that fieldnotes are always selective and that where they have not been written on the spot, as is common, we must consider the possible distortions of memory. By contrast, transcripts of audio- or video-recordings have the advantage that they will usually be more accurate and fuller in reporting what was said than fieldnotes. However, they do not record everything, and even transcripts are constructions: they involve assumptions of various kinds, for example about who was speaking to whom (Ochs 1979, Atkinson 1992). Furthermore, what are presented in ethnographic accounts are *extracts* from fieldnotes or transcripts, and so we must bear in mind the process of selection at this level too, and the possible relevance of what is not quoted.

Besides features of the research process, we also need to take account of what we know about the ethnographer, and the resulting potential for biases of various kinds. For instance, if we are looking at a study of political influence on the presentation of news in the mass media and we know that the researcher was commissioned by a news organisation, or (conversely) that he or she is a well-known critic of the media, we ought to be on the lookout for the sorts of potential bias that these identities imply. Here, of course, research biographies are often an important source of information. This is not a matter of dismissing what is claimed on the grounds that the researcher is biased, but rather of taking the possibility of bias into account in our assessment.

Informants' accounts may take the form of interview responses, documents of various kinds, and even of accounts given by one participant to another that were overheard by the researcher.

All three sources of error that I identified as operating on observers' reports must also be considered in relation to informants' accounts. Thus, in assessing them we need to consider the possible effects of the informant's presence and role on what was observed. (Unless the informant is very closely associated with the research the greatest danger here will be personal rather than procedural reactivity.) Second, we must assess the nature of the phenomenon being described and the implications of this for the likelihood of error. The third source of error, the reporting process itself, is more complex in the case of informants' accounts. We must note whether the account is a first-hand report on the part of the informant, or a report of what others have told the informant about what they saw or heard. Evidence of the latter kind is especially problematic, since we will not know what distortions may have occurred in the passage of information to the informant. It should also be borne in mind that informants are likely to rely on memory rather than fieldnotes or audio-recording, so that there is more scope for memory distortion.

In addition to assessing the threats to validity operating on the information available to the informant, we must also consider those that relate to the transmission of information from informant to ethnographer. For example, we must assess the effects of the context in which the informant's account was elicited: for what audience (interviewer and/or others), in response to what stimulus, with what purposes in mind, under what constraints, and so on. Also, what threats to validity may have been operative on the ethnographer's recording and interpretation of the informant's account? Such accounts may be recorded in fieldnote form or by audio-recording; and all the considerations I outlined earlier in relation to these forms of recording apply here too. Finally, once again, it must be remembered that what are made available in ethnographic research reports are selections from informants' accounts, and so we must bear in mind the possible relevance of what was left out for our interpretation of the extracts presented in research reports.

Claims may also sometimes be supported by references to published sources of various kinds: whether other research reports, official documents, newspaper articles, personal diaries or auto-biographies, even fictional accounts. Thus, for example, in his discussion of Edinburgh medical students' judgements of clinical units, Atkinson appeals for support to Becker and Geer's study of local medical student culture in a North American hospital (Atkinson 1981a:23, Becker *et al.* 1961). And earlier, in his discussion of the division between pre-clinical and clinical phases of medical education and the malaise it can cause among students, he cites the report of the Royal Commission on Medical Education (Atkinson 1981a:17). Elsewhere, he draws on a novel by Richard Gordon to illustrate the nature of bedside teaching (Atkinson 1975). References to published sources can be used both as a basis for inferences about the features of their author(s) (these perhaps representing some relevant category of personnel) and as accounts telling us about the phenomena to which they refer. That is, they may be used in ways analogous both to observers' reports and to informants' accounts.

How much reliance we place on such published evidence involves difficult judgements. After all, it may involve all the sorts of potential threats to validity that can apply to any research report. And we should remember that authors' references to sources are not always accurate. Judgement should depend greatly on the nature of the source itself (as far as we can judge this) and the purpose for which it is being used. Where it is related to a central claim, it may be necessary to examine the source for oneself.

Another kind of evidence that may be provided in support of descriptions (and sometimes also of explanations) is that arising from what is referred to as respondent validation. Here the ethnographic account is presented to the people (or more usually to some of the people) to whom it refers, and their judgements about its validity reported. Sometimes this seems to be taken as the litmus test of validity in ethnographic research (see, for example, Lincoln and Guba 1985). However, while such evidence is of value, it cannot be treated as providing a definitive test of validity unless we assume that participants both know (or can recognise) with certainty the relevant facts about their situation and behaviour *and* are able and willing to admit such facts. There seem to me to be no good reasons for adopting either of these assumptions in a blanket fashion. Whether they are reasonable will depend on the nature of the claim and of the participant and her or his circumstances. The same sceptical approach should be applied to such data as to all informant accounts, it seems to me.

A useful form of check on the validity of descriptive claims that ethnographers sometimes employ is triangulation. This can take a variety of forms, but the principle involved is simple. If we accept that all kinds of data involve potential threats to validity, and that these may differ in likelihood across data types and sources, then by comparing data carrying different validity threats we may be able to make a more effective assessment of the likely truth of the claim. Explicit examples of triangulation are rare in ethnographic studies. One example, though, is provided by Lever (1981). This arises from her research on sex differences in children's play, where she compares questionnaire and diary data. What is hoped for in triangulation, of course, is that the different data sources will confirm one another. But, frequently, this does not happen; and, in fact, Lever found that the questionnaire data showed stronger sex differences in play activities than did the diary reports. Faced with such a discrepancy, the researcher and the reader must try to make some assessment of the reasons for it, so that a conclusion can be reached about which finding is most likely to be true. Lever argues that the discrepancy in her study arose from the fact that questionnaire data probably tend to elicit responses that are more influenced by a person's perceptions of social norms than are diary entries; and so she concludes that the latter are the more accurate. As readers, we must consider the plausibility of this argument, both in itself and in comparison with others that point in a different direction. For example, might it be the case that the diary entries covered a shorter period of time and were not representative of the usual patterns, whereas the questionnaire data drew on the children's own greater experience of what they typically do? It should be noted that such issues arise even where the different data sources confirm one another. We must ask whether these sources might have shared some common source of error that would explain their similar results, so that they may both be wrong.

In this section I have considered assessment of the validity of evidential claims in their own terms. Equally important, though, is whether, and how strongly, they support the major claims for which they are used as evidence.

The relationship between evidence and claim   The evidence may seem quite plausible and/or credible in itself, and yet the support it offers for the claim may be questionable. Take, for example, the following extract dealing with the adaptations of female factory workers to their work:

'Cutting off', or separating, the 'inner self' from what is objectively happening on the 'outside' is one of the sorry 'skills' we are forced into, in an existence dominated by alienated relations of production. It is otherwise known as 'wishing one's life away'. Some girls actually prided themselves in the art of switching off, pitying those who were bad at it, and thinking themselves lucky to be working at all:

> Racquel: Yes, you get bored sitting up here, very bored ... You gets used to it, though. I think it's imagination a lot of the time. I get fed up sometimes, but I don't really get that fed up, because I haven't really got anything to be fed up about.
> Anna (the researcher): What do you think about?
> Racquel: Nothing, really. I can sit up here a whole day without really speaking.

> (Pollert 1981:131)

Here the evidence offered takes the form of an informant's account of her life at work. It is not clear whether the extract is from fieldnotes or from audio-recording, but either way there is no obvious reason to doubt that it is an accurate representation of what was said. However, a serious question does arise about the relationship of this evidence to the multiple claims the author makes in the discussion that precedes the quotation. These claims are

- that the workers cut themselves off or switch off from their work;
- that they refer to this as 'wishing one's life away'; and that it is a 'sorry' skill produced by alienated relations of production;
- that some of the women prided themselves on their ability to switch off, and pitied those who were bad at it, judging themselves lucky to be working.

The quotation supports the first claim (assuming that this worker is typical of the rest). However, it provides no evidence for the other two claims. What this indicates is that we must look carefully at the relationship between evidence and claims: the evidence may give only partial support for the set of claims that the author is presenting.

Sometimes, too, one finds that there are alternative plausible interpretations of the evidence that would not support the claim. Take the following example, also from Pollert's study. Here the evidence quoted is intended to support the argument that 'supervision was sexually oppressive' and that the women were forced into a 'defensive–aggressive strategy' on the men's terms:

On one occasion one of the ... girls was 'messing around' and was wheeled off to a lift on a trolley by a young man. Everybody joined in the joke:

> Kathy: It weren't my fault. (shrieking)
> Steven (Chargehand): What are you up to? It's your sexy looks that always does it.
> Brenda (looking on, and giving a husky laugh): Watch him back there! Oh! – I wouldn't trust him!

There was no way the chargehand could have broken up the general 'laugh' without antagonising the girls. So he diffused it with jocular flattery, never even approaching the young man who was responsible. The girl returned to work, put in her place; but instead of sheepishly acknowledging his authority, was able to continue giggling, as if to demonstrate she did not feel humiliated.

(Pollert 1981:143)

It is possible that this is indeed an example of sexual oppression, and that the participation of the women was 'a defensive–aggressive strategy' on the men's terms that they were 'forced into'. Clearly Pollert is drawing on considerable experience of life in the factory she describes. However, this evidence is not entirely convincing support for her claim. There are elements of it which suggest a different, equally plausible interpretation. There is no clear indication that the men started this incident or that they transformed what had already begun into something else. While the author suggests that 'the young man' was responsible, it is not clear on what basis this judgement was made; and given its evaluative nature I think we must suspend judgement about it. Furthermore, Pollert reports that 'everyone joined in the joke' and that it was a 'general laugh' which the chargehand could not have broken up without antagonising the women. These features might be taken to suggest a process of joking around that both sexes found congenial, especially as a break from work.

Pollert claims that the woman was 'put in her place' and humiliated by the chargehand, and that her response was designed to disguise this. But this is an especially difficult sort of interpretation to establish. We cannot assume that all women would always be humiliated by such 'jocular flattery'. No doubt some would, under some circumstances. But what evidence is there to suggest that this is a case in point? This is not the kind of description that one can read off from an observation with minimal danger of misinterpretation. At the very least, some account from the women involved in this incident is required.

An additional problem is that it is not even very clear what would count as sexual oppression, neither the intension nor extension of this concept is well-defined. While core examples are fairly obvious, the boundaries are unclear, and this example is outside that core, it seems to me. Furthermore, much to her credit, Pollert makes her own feminist views quite explicit at the beginning of her book (Pollert 1981:2). Given these views, and presuming that they predated the research, we can suspect that she may have been predisposed to find such oppression. This might lead her to detect examples that others, such as non-feminists and men, would miss. Equally, though, it might also lead her to misinterpret some incidents as sexually oppressive that were not. As readers we have to make a judgement on the evidence that she provides, and our judgements will of course reflect our own views and experience to some degree. What is essential, though, is that we strive to find common ground for such judgements, and for me Pollert does not succeed in finding it in this case.[5]

The problem of the relationship between evidence and claim may also arise where appeal is made to published sources. For example, when Parker *et al.* appeal to a national study of magistrates to support their claim about the middle-class background of magistrates at Countyside (Parker *et al.* 1981:89), we must ask whether we can be confident about inferring from the findings of that study to the situation at Countyside. The relationship may turn out to be convincing, but the issue must be addressed.

Description of larger scale phenomena

Let us now broaden our focus to look at descriptions of larger geographical and/or temporal phenomena that cannot be observed by an ethnographer or informant in one go. Here the claim (explicitly or implicitly) will involve a synthesis of multiple judgements and probably also generalisation from what was observed to what was not. Most claims in ethnographic research reports are of this kind; indeed, many of those discussed in the previous section effectively fall into this category. Often there are generalisations across a population of participants in a setting, as when Parker *et al.* make claims about all or most of the magistrates working in Countyside Court on the basis of evidence presented about the attitudes and actions of a few of them. Simultaneously, there may also be generalisation over time, so that Parker *et al.*'s claim that magistrates at Countyside espoused a criminal family thesis was not a claim about what magistrates believed at one brief point in time but rather about what was assumed to be a stable feature of their behaviour over the whole period of observation, and perhaps beyond.

Occasionally, such generalisation is plausible or credible at face value, but often we may need evidence to establish that what is true of the instance described is likely to be true of others within the case. And where such evidence is not available we must suspend judgement. Thus, it seems to me that Parker *et al.* do not establish that all or even a majority of Countyside magistrates were committed to the criminal families thesis, nor that it was a stable feature of their orientation over time.

Sometimes, generalisations within the case studied may be supported by data about multiple instances, perhaps even reports about the precise frequency of the relevant events. This may take the form of information about the frequency with which a particular sort of opinion was expressed across a population of informants. Equally, it may be a report about the frequency of the relevant sort of event over time. An example of the latter is to be found in Pollard's (1984) study of the effects of classroom regime on the differentiation of pupils. He argues that traditional forms of teaching tend to result in friendships among children being correlated with academic achievement levels. In seeking to document the differences in teaching style between the two teachers he studied, Pollard provides a table that reports the frequency of different sorts of contact between them and their pupils (see Table 1).

Table 1 **Teacher–child contacts %**

| | Child initiated | | Teacher initiated | | |
	Work-related	Other	Work-related	Other	Advisory
Mrs Rothwell's class	12	15	27	11	35
Mr Harman's class	20	32	18	17	13

(Adapted from Pollard 1984, p. 36)

It is certainly of great value to have evidence of this kind. It provides much more of a basis on which to judge the soundness of the generalisation than where the writer simply asserts that such and such frequently happened or was generally true. However, such evidence must still be handled carefully; questions may need to be asked about it. In the case of Pollard's data, I think we need to know:

1. The period over which the observation of teacher–pupil contacts was carried out; whether it was continuous; and its size relative to the time-span over which generalisation is being made.

2. How rigorously teacher–child contacts were identified. Variations in identification procedure over the course of observation are a potential source of error and we need to know how large this error might be. This covers both the question of how clear and concrete the identification criteria were and how effectively, practically speaking, these criteria were applied. For example, was the coding done on the spot in the classroom or on the basis of a video recording? This might make a difference to the level of error. On the one hand, video-recording might reduce the likelihood of error in recording the data; on the other, it may imply a higher level of procedural reactivity.

3. How rigorously were the child–teacher initiative and work-related/other/advisory distinctions made? Again, we need to know how closely specified the categories were and how effective the counting of instances was, given practical constraints.

Numerical frequencies should not be taken as self-evident proof of generalisability, then. While they provide us with more of a basis for assessing generalisations across people and/or over time than informal judgements about these matters, threats to their validity must still be addressed.

In this section I have looked at the assessment of descriptions, both of small and of larger scale phenomena. This requires examining the plausibility and/or credibility of the claims and of any evidence provided in their support. In the case of evidence, we must consider the likely validity both of the evidential claims themselves and of the inferences from evidence back to claim. Finally, I looked at the problem of generalising within the case, the sorts of evidence that are used to support such generalisations and the considerations that must be borne in mind in assessing them.

Explanations

As I noted in Chapter 2, all types of claim (except definitions) include a descriptive component. Given this, a first step in assessing the validity of explanations is to identify and assess their component descriptions, explicit or implicit. This is done in precisely the same way as one assesses any other description. Over and above this, though, we must look at how well the evidence supports the specifically explanatory element of the claim. There are two steps in this process. First, all explanations involve theoretical assumptions and it is necessary to assess the validity of these. Second, it must be shown that the explanation fits the case at least as well as any competing alternative.

An example

To illustrate the assessment of explanations I want to look again at the extract from Parker *et al.*'s study of juvenile courts that I discussed in Chapter 2. You may remember that their aim in that extract was to explain why the sentencing in Countyside Court was more punitive than at City Court. They argue that this cannot be simply because there was a social class differential between magistrates and offenders. The critical factor, they argue, was the relative absence of institutionalised procedures within Countyside Court that would have minimised the effects of what they see as the inappropriate social class-based assumptions held by magistrates, as they did at City Court. I will look first at the descriptive claims involved in this argument, and then at assessment of the explanatory component.

Descriptive claims   There are several descriptive claims involved in this explanation:

1. That justice at Countyside Court is more punitive than at City Court.
2. That there is a sharp social class differential between magistrates and offenders in both courts.
3. That the court officials' assumption that there was an underclass of criminal families in Countyside was false.
4. That procedures of 'due process' and so on were less operative at Countyside than at City Court.

Descriptive claim 1. This is the description of the phenomenon to be explained. As we noted earlier, it is slightly ambiguous. It looks like a value claim: that justice at Countyside is unfair. And, indeed,

I think it does have this character. However, it is also factual: it implies that cases of the same sort incurred more severe sentences at Countyside than at City. And this forms the basis for a major factual claim of the book as a whole:

> ...we find that juveniles from the same backgrounds ..., charged with similar offences, are subjected to quite different court regimes, and receive widely divergent sentences, which have major and wide-ranging effects on their lives.
>
> (Parker *et al.* 1981:22)

Clearly, this is not an argument that is immediately convincing in itself: it is not so plausible that we do not need to consider its credibility. Nor, in my judgement, is it credible as it stands; since it involves complex judgements comparing individual cases with respect to the defendants' backgrounds, the offences committed, and the relative severity of the sentences handed down. Furthermore, I think we need evidence about the validity of the generalisation from the cases discussed to all those occurring at Countyside in the relevant period.

Parker *et al.* do provide some evidence for this claim in the extract included in Chapter 2, though it is not explicitly presented for this purpose. They claim that 'Fines tend to be comparatively high' (p. 89); and they report two instances of the use of compensation orders that they regard as severe and that were quashed by the Crown Court (see p. 39 above).

The first of these evidential claims involves generalisation and comparison (presumably with City Court), but the basis for neither is indicated. In my judgement, the complex nature of this claim means that it cannot be accepted without further supporting evidence, and none is provided.

The other two items of evidence are more specific. For the most part I think that we can accept the validity of the evidence itself. The only exception is the suggestion that 'because the presiding magistrates went out of their way to state, quite unsolicited, that the compensation had absolutely nothing to do with the car being a Daimler' (p. 89) we can infer that the make of car did have an effect on the level of compensation.[6] We are all aware that people do not always tell the truth, and are not even always aware of their own motivations; and this seems as likely to be true of magistrates as of anyone else. However, when we take what people say as implying the converse, we must surely provide evidence. Since the authors offer no evidence, I think we must suspend judgement about the validity of this particular argument. The rest of the evidence, however, seems credible at face value.

More problematic is the relationship between this evidence and the claim that these two cases are instances of relatively punitive justice. As with the general statement about the comparatively high level of fines, here too issues of comparison and generalisation are involved for which we need evidence; but, again, none is provided.

Earlier in their book Parker *et al.* provide some other evidence for the claim that justice at Countyside is comparatively punitive, in the form of data on the proportions of various types of disposal at Countyside compared with City Court, all courts in the same metropolitan region, and all juvenile courts in England and Wales. I have summarised these data in Figure 2.

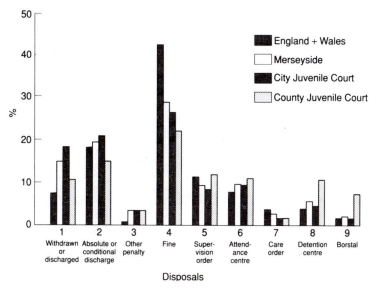

Figure 2

These data show clearly that the proportion of more severe sentences (detention centre and borstal recommendation) is higher at Countyside Court than elsewhere. This is certainly stronger evidence than that available in the extract, and provides a useful complement to it. However, there are reasons why even this evidence could be misleading. For instance, there may be something about the cases that Countyside Court deals with that explains the different profile of disposals there. Are there more recidivists, or are the offences typically more serious, and so on? Indeed, if the Countyside magistrates were right and there was an underclass of criminal families in their area, but not in City, then this might explain the deviant pattern of disposals at Countyside. This is such an important claim in the context of Parker *et al.*'s study that I think we need more information before we can make a reasonable judgement.

Descriptive claim 2. This second claim relates to one of the factors held to explain the punitive character of justice at Countyside. And it seems to me that the argument that there is a social class differential between magistrates and defendants is quite plausible as it stands. On the basis of everyday knowledge I think we can accept that the magistrates at Countyside were probably middle-class and that since the working class are disproportionately represented among defendants in juvenile courts this was probably the case at Countyside. These seem reasonable conclusions, despite their probabilistic character and the vagueness of the terms 'middle class' and 'working class'. The authors also offer some evidence in support of this claim, which adds further to its plausibility.

Descriptive claim 3. We cannot accept this claim as plausible or credible at face value, but the authors do provide some evidence. They test the criminal families thesis against information about the frequency with which the same names recurred on the Countyside juvenile court records over the year during which they carried out their observations. From this they conclude that the thesis was false. However, in my view a year is likely to be too short a time to pick up a pattern of recurring names. Five or six years might have been a more convincing test. I think we have to suspend judgement about the validity of this claim.

Descriptive claim 4. This claim refers to what the authors take to be the key element in the explanation of the punitive character of Countyside justice. It is a comparative claim about the relationship between proceedings in City and Countyside Courts. Elsewhere in their book, the authors describe the legal process in City Court as characterised by operational but unwritten rules that have become normative over time, having the following three features:

1. Due process is adhered to most of the time and even on those occasions when it was deviated from this did not seem to go against the offenders' interests.[7] Thus, court personnel took great care to explain the charge and to elicit the correct plea by talking to both juvenile and parent(s). 70% of offenders had legal representation and this was encouraged, only 4% of applications for legal aid were refused.
2. Civil treatment of offenders and their families was the norm.
3. The full tariff of sentences was used, usually proceeding up the ladder of severity of disposal one step at a time.

(Parker *et al.* 1981:ch. 4)

By contrast, the authors claim that at Countyside Court due process was more frequently 'interpreted', either to serve the interests of court personnel or 'to inflict moral or social stigma upon defendants and parents'. Thus, there was 'not much attempt to explain jargon and check that the defendant understood what is going on' (Parker *et al.* 1981:82). Defendants and their families were 'herded' into court and the charge read without much allowance for questions. Also, there was a failure to offer defendants basic courtesy, and extraneous material was introduced that was insulting and stigmatising. Furthermore, the Court tended to accept a defendant's desire to proceed without legal representation rather than urging the desirability of representation; and it refused a higher level of applications for legal aid than did City. There was also a failure to give reasons, either for the refusal of aid or for the sentences given. Finally, Countyside Court magistrates used a short tariff, moving quite quickly to severe punishments (Parker *et al.* 1981:ch. 5).

This claim and its components cannot be accepted as sufficiently plausible at face value; nor is its credibility sufficient, since multiple and comparative judgements are involved as well as generalisations over time. We require further evidence, I think. The authors recognise this and provide a considerable amount of it. For the most part, though, it is concerned with the attitudes of the magistrates and court officials as these are revealed by what is said and done in court (and in interviews), rather than with showing that due process was not adhered to, and that magistrates did not make use of the full tariff. What this evidence does support, to some degree, is that officials were sometimes uncivil to defendants and to their parents; though even here we are given little contextual information by which we can check this interpretation, and it is not clear how representative of court process at Countyside such examples of incivility were.

Explanatory claims   Where, as in this case, we have found one or more of the descriptive claims involved in an explanation to be unconvincing, the explanation as a whole cannot be convincing. However, it is still worth considering the level of conviction that we should have in the *explanatory* component of Parker *et al.*'s argument. The explanation that these authors put forward has two links

1. That the social class background of City and Countyside magistrates gives them false (or otherwise inappropriate) assumptions about defendants and their families.

2. That the relative absence of institutionalised procedures imple-
    menting due process and so on led to these inappropriate
    assumptions influencing court decisions and thereby producing
    relatively punitive justice at Countyside.

Explanatory claim 1.[8] In assessing an explanatory claim we must
begin, I suggested, by considering the theoretical assumption on
which it is based. Here, the general idea seems to be that people's
social class background affects how they see the world and may
lead to erroneous views about the lives of people in other social
classes. In my judgement this is quite plausible enough to accept as
a theoretical principle. As regards its plausibility as an explanation
of events at Countyside, we should note that we have accepted that
there does seem likely to have been a social class differential
between magistrates and defendants there, so that the conditions
for the application of this theoretical principle are met. On the
other hand, we saw that the claim that the magistrates' attitudes
were false or inappropriate had not been established. Furthermore,
the validity of this explanation in relation to alternatives is not
assessed. And the claim that the criminal families thesis and other
attitudes that Countyside magistrates display are characteristically
middle-class is not entirely convincing. Age or generation might be
factors of at least equal importance. This first explanatory argument is not entirely convincing, then.

Explanatory claim 2. The theoretical assumption presupposed by
this explanation seems to be that unless constrained by institutional
procedures, inappropriate assumptions about others will result in
relatively severe treatment of them (compared to people of one's
own class or group). This also seems reasonably plausible. We are
all aware of how ethnocentrism of one kind or another can blind us
to the problems that other people face, and so lead us to unfair
treatment. Once again, though, we must ask whether it seems likely
in this case that the phenomena being explained would not have
occurred without the effect of the explanatory factor cited. My
major doubt about this explanation concerns the question of
why the institutionalised procedures operated at City but not at
Countyside. This is especially important because it seems plausible
that the relative weakness of institutionalised procedures and the
severe sentencing at Countyside could both have been products of
some other factor, rather than the former causing the latter.

What all this suggests, I think, is that we need a good deal more
evidence before we should be convinced that Parker *et al.*'s
explanatory argument is valid. However, whether or not you agree
with this judgement, I hope that the discussion has given you a

sense of what is involved in assessing explanatory claims. As I suggested earlier, we cannot expect that there will always be a consensus in judgements about validity, not even after detailed discussion; but this does not deny the possibility of rational assessment or that consensus can often be reached.

The assessment of explanations, then, involves all the considerations that I outlined in discussing descriptions, plus distinctive issues concerning their specifically explanatory element. The latter, like the former, requires us to make judgements about what is plausible and credible, judgements that can be reasonable or unreasonable but whose validity or invalidity we can never know with absolute certainty.

A note on assessing evaluations

In addition to descriptive and explanatory claims, ethnographers also sometimes make evaluations. We can adopt different attitudes towards these. We could leave them on one side as inappropriate in a research context, restricting our attention to their factual elements. Alternatively, we can consider how reasonable the evaluation is, while recognising that researchers have no distinctive authority in this area. This would involve considering both what values have and have not been, should and should not have been, taken into account in the value judgement; and how those values have been interpreted in their application to the particular phenomena concerned.

As an illustration of how one might set about assessing evaluations in ethnographic research, let me return again to the study of juvenile courts by Parker *et al.* In its overall conception, this was an explicitly evaluative study. The authors were concerned to test the quality of the justice dispensed by City and Countyside Courts. I have already dealt with the descriptive and explanatory components of their argument, so I will concentrate here on the evaluative element. To begin with we must ask what values underly their evaluation. Fairly obviously, the key value is justice, but there are several aspects of this value mentioned by the authors. First, this value is taken to imply that, in formal terms, there should be consistency of treatment within the same court over time and between courts, so that the same kinds of cases are treated in the same way. Second, the authors distinguish between two bases on which judgements about the equivalence of cases can be made, and they advocate one of these over the other. On the one hand, natural justice involves taking account of such things as the seriousness of the offence and the previous record of the defendant, abstracting offenders and offences from the rest of their social context. What the authors call 'social justice', on the other hand, takes account of some of the social (including material) circumstances of the offender; so that, for example, family poverty might be a basis for mitigating sentences where it was judged a contributory factor to the offence.

The first of these standards of assessment (consistency of treatment) seems acceptable as it stands and therefore not in need of justification, though judgements about the equivalence of cases, about levels of seriousness of offences, and the significance of previous record, could vary. The second, advocacy of social justice, is more controversial. While it is certainly not an unreasonable concept, it is not the one that is institutionalised in the courts, and it has been the subject of much debate. Given this, we need some supporting argument as to why it is to be preferred over natural justice. And part of that discussion should probably deal with the problems that might arise if that concept of justice were adopted by the courts, and how those problems could be dealt with. For example, how would magistrates assess poverty and what degree of mitigation should be involved. Parker *et al.* provide some justificatory argument in support of the concept of social justice, though in my view they do not deal with all the questions that require treatment (Parker *et al.* 1981:246–7).

Assessing the conclusions drawn

In Chapter 2, I drew a distinction between the main claims of an ethnographic account (which relate to the case studied), and the conclusions drawn on the basis of those claims (which relate to the focus of the research). Sometimes, there may be no separate focus, and therefore no conclusions beyond the main claims. Most ethnographic studies, though, do draw or imply such conclusions. Thus, having assessed the main arguments of a study, we will often have to give separate consideration to its conclusions. Usually, what this will involve is assessing the basis on which inferences from claim to conclusion were made. Earlier, I identified two strategies by which ethnographers seek to draw such inferences: theoretical inference and empirical generalisation. Here I want to look at how we assess examples of each of these types of conclusion.

Theoretical inference

Theoretical claims are distinctive in that they are universal in scope: they refer to a probably infinite range of possible cases (those where the conditions are met) rather than specifically to a finite set of actual cases. What we must assess here, then, is the extent to which evidence about the case(s) studied can provide a basis for such universal claims.

We should begin by recognising that there is one sense in which no basis for universal claims can be made: evidence about a finite number of particular cases can never allow us to draw conclusions on a strictly logical basis (that is, with complete certainty) about a universal. This is known as the problem of induction. Various attempts have been made to find some logical basis for induction, but it is widely agreed that none of these have been successful (Popper 1959, Newton-Smith 1981). However, once we abandon the idea that a claim to validity must be certain beyond all possible doubt before we can call it knowledge, and accept that we can distinguish between claims that are more or less likely to be true, the problem of induction becomes less severe (though still not easy to deal with). In short, once we adopt a subtle realism we can, in principle at least, draw reasonable conclusions about theoretical claims.

One of the problems with the concept of theoretical inference is that it has been interpreted in several (often not clearly distinguished) ways by ethnographers (Hammersley 1989 and 1992:ch. 5). One approach that has been designed to lay the basis for the development and testing of theory is what is sometimes referred to as analytic induction (Znaniecki 1934, Lindesmith 1937 and 1968, Cressey 1953). While explicit use of this approach has become relatively rare in recent times, it is nevertheless instructive.

Cressey's study of embezzlement is one of the best examples of analytical induction. His central question was: under what conditions do people take the decision to embezzle? In developing and testing his theory Cressey studied a large number of cases, interviewing people who had been convicted of embezzlement and other forms of 'financial trust violation'. His final formulation was that:

Trusted persons become trust violators when they conceive of themselves as having a financial problem which is non-shareable, have the knowledge or awareness that this problem can be secretly resolved by violation of the position of financial trust, and are able to apply to their own conduct in that situation verbalizations that enable them to adjust their conceptions of themselves as trusted persons with their conceptions of themselves as users of the entrusted funds or property.

(Cressey 1950:742)

During the course of his research Cressey reformulated his theory several times in the face of falsifying evidence. And, indeed, in its final form, it seems plausible and credible on the basis of the evidence he supplies. However, it is important to notice that cases were selected for investigation on the basis that they exhibited the phenomenon the theory was designed to explain (embezzlement). As Robinson (1951) points out, there was no investigation of cases where the factors assumed to cause embezzlement were present, in order to discover whether it always (or more frequently) occurred in those cases. What this suggests is that research concerned with developing and testing theory requires that we investigate cases where the theoretical variable takes contrasting values, with a view to finding out if the phenomenon being explained varies in the way that the theory would lead us to expect. Also required is that the cases should be such that relevant extraneous variables (those which might also produce the phenomenon being investigated) are controlled (that is, kept at the same level or minimised). These features are largely absent from Cressey's study.[9] The only ethnographic research of which I am aware that approximates to this model is the series of studies by Hargreaves (1967), Lacey (1970) and Ball (1981). This research involved the development and testing of differentiation-polarisation theory: the claim that differentiation of pupils on academic–behavioural grounds produces polarisation in their attitudes towards school.[10]

This sequence of studies began with an investigation of a secondary modern school, where the researcher can have had little doubt that polarisation of attitudes would be found. Differentiation-polarisation theory was presented as applying to processes in the school at two levels. First, at the organisational level, it was claimed that the streaming of pupils produced a polarisation in their perspectives between top and bottom streams (the former predominantly pro-school, the latter predominantly anti-school), with the middle two streams occupying an intermediate position. Second, it was suggested that differentiation within classes produced intra-class polarisation of attitude, with those placed at the top of the class being pro-school and those at the bottom anti-school. Hargreaves uses a simple diagram to illustrate the combined effect of these two differentiation-polarisation processes in the secondary modern school he studied (see Figure 3).

I will focus on differentiation-polarisation theory as it applies at the organisational level, since this is the form in which the theory has been developed and tested most effectively. In these terms, what Hargreaves' study amounts to is the description of a case where differentiation was high and so too was polarisation. Useful though this is, it is obviously rather weak evidence for the validity of the theory. After all, many other factors were likely to have been

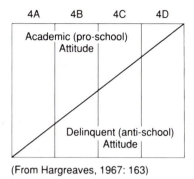

(From Hargreaves, 1967: 163)

Figure 3 **Representation of two subcultures**

operative in the situation, some of which may well have produced the high level of polarisation. For instance, perhaps the streaming system in the school Hargreaves studied sorted pupils on the basis of their attitude to school: both directly because this was judged to be an important consideration by teachers, and indirectly because attitude had affected past academic performance. Differences in pupil attitude produced by factors outside the school could therefore explain the correlation between stream and orientation to school that Hargreaves found.

If we turn now to Lacey's study, we can see how it contributes to the process of testing the theory. Not only does he document much the same correlation between stream and attitude as Hargreaves, but:

1. The case he studied involved some control over the factor of differences among pupils in attitude on entry to the school. This is because Hightown was a selective school, so most of the pupils who were recruited to it had been successful and highly motivated in their primary schools.
2. He shows that the polarisation increased over time from the point of initial differentiation in the first year through to the fourth year of secondary schooling.

This certainly adds considerably to the credibility of the theory, though. It does not render it completely convincing. As regards the first feature of Lacey's study, we must remember that differences in attitude are a matter of degree. Despite relative homogeneity in comparison with differences in attitude across the whole age group, there will still have been some differences among the new recruits to Hightown, and the streaming system may simply have allocated pupils to streams on that basis. Similarly, we could explain the growing polarisation over time not as the product of differentiation but as the result of external factors operating on existing differences in attitude. After all, a lot of things happen to pupils during their secondary school careers, both changes in relationships at home and in peer groups; and some of these are likely to be systematically related to attitude towards school.[11]

In the third of this sequence of studies, Ball investigated a comprehensive school. As a result of this choice of school type he was not able to control for pupils' attitude on entry in the way that Lacey did. However, he did look at change in pupils' attitudes over time, confirming Lacey's findings. Furthermore, he was able to document a change in the level of differentiation in the institution (the abandonment of banding in favour of mixed ability grouping), looking at the effects of this on the level of polarisation. Given that this involved a change within a single institution we can assume that much (though not everything) remained the same between the two situations, before and after.[12] Ball shows that the level of polarisation was much lower after mixed ability grouping had been adopted.

This is further important evidence in support of differentiation-polarisation theory, but once again it is not beyond reasonable question. It does not rule out all the other relevant possibilities. For example, the data produced by these studies could be explained by a kind of imitation theory whereby the attitudes of members of a school class are affected by the balance of extant pro- and anti-school attitudes to be found within it, a theory that some teachers hold. This would explain the reduction of polarisation following the abolition of banding independently of level of differentiation.

Whatever the remaining questions, this sequence of studies is one of the clearest examples of systematic theory development and testing in ethnographic research, and indeed in sociology generally. It illustrates what is required but rarely done, and as such it provides a standard against which we can compare studies that claim to draw theoretical conclusions.[13]

As we saw in Chapter 2, ethnographic studies do often claim that the case studied is crucial for some theory. However, sometimes the theory involved is not well defined (being mixed up with descriptive and explanatory arguments) and the critical character of the case is not always clearly established. Woods' work on course choice in a secondary school, and the effects of examination pressure on this, involves a relatively clear specification of why the case studied is of critical importance for the theory (see Chapter 2, Woods 1979a and b). Even here, though, there are serious problems. First, he does not provide evidence to establish the critical nature of the case: comparatively speaking, how heavy was the pressure on this school to achieve good examination results? If the school were not distinctive in this respect, and other schools under greater pressure gave greater choice, this would throw doubt on the theory. Second, Woods does not give attention to other factors that might have produced limited course choice for pupils. Perhaps because of a rather traditional orientation the teachers had never been committed to giving pupils a wide range of choice? Perhaps resource limitations were very severe and this limited choice?

It is worth reiterating, though, that there are problems with the very notion of theory. Few ethnographers today believe that universal laws of human behaviour exist. They argue that human actions are not causally determined, or at least not fully determined, and do not conform to lawlike patterns (Blumer 1939 and 1969, Matza 1964 and 1969). If this is true, the strategy I outlined above may not be an appropriate model for theoretical inference. And on this basis some would deny that studies like those of Cressey and Hargreaves/Lacey/Ball produce either new theoretical ideas or ideas that are more precise or better established than those which are routinely used in sociological explanations. Yet it is not clear what the alternative to this approach is (Hammersley 1989).

Empirical generalisation

The other way in which ethnographers may seek to draw conclusions about their research focus from their findings about the case(s) studied is empirical generalisation. Here the aim is to generalise. to some larger whole or aggregate of cases of which the cases studied form part. A first requirement in assessing such generalisations is to know the identity of the larger aggregate. As I noted in Chapter 2, this is not always made explicit by authors. Similarly, it is not always clear on what grounds the author believes that the case(s) studied are typical of the larger population. In the absence of such information the reader must try to judge what the most likely population is, and consider the probable validity of generalisation to that population on this basis.

It is important not to see statistical sampling techniques as the only way in which empirical generalisations can be made.[14] It is very rare that these techniques can be used in ethnographic research since the size of the sample of cases is not usually large enough. However, there are various sorts of evidence that ethnographers can use to support empirical generalisation. Thus, it may be possible to draw on relevant information in published statistics about the aggregate to which generalisation is being made. So, Parker *et al.* used statistics about the proportions of different sorts of disposal in juvenile courts in England and Wales and the Merseyside area to show the atypicality of Countyside, and these data also establish the relative typicality (in this respect) of City Court. Similarly, where other studies have been carried out on other cases in the same population in the same time period comparison may allow some judgement of typicality to be made. An example is provided by Strong (1979) in his study of paediatric consultations. He argues that the bureaucratic format he identified is not just typical of such consultations but that (with minor modifications) it also predominates in all medical consultations in the British health service. In order to establish this he first considers the extent to which the fact that children were the patients in the paediatric consultations he studied shaped the ceremonial order characteristic of them, arguing that it made little difference. Second, he draws on other studies of medical consultation involving adults as patients to assess how far these conformed to the bureaucratic mode.

There is no doubt that ethnographic studies can, and probably already do, provide descriptive information about settings that are typical in relevant respects of larger aggregates that are of interest to us. However, in general ethnographers are not very effective in establishing the typicality of what they report. And in the absence of such information we must often suspend judgement about the generalisability of their claims.[15]

Conclusion

In this chapter we have looked at assessing the validity of the major claims, the evidence for them, and the conclusions presented in ethnographic accounts. The starting point for such assessments is the plausibility of the claims in terms of the reader's background knowledge. I argued in Chapter 3 that the level of plausibility required by researchers should be higher, on average, than that demanded by others. However, there will be many (usually evidential rather than major) claims that can be reasonably judged to be sufficiently plausible as they stand to be acceptable. A second test is of credibility: the reader must judge the likelihood of error given the danger of reactivity, the nature of the feature about which claims are being made, the circumstances under which the research was carried out, and what is known about the researcher. Where the claim is judged to be neither sufficiently plausible or credible, any evidence offered in support of it must be considered, and if none is available then the validity of the claim should be judged uncertain. In assessing the evidence offered we must take account of the type of claim involved, since different types of claim require different kinds of evidence. All claims involve descriptions and here we must assess both the validity of the evidence itself and the strength of the inference from evidence to claim. Also, any generalisations within the case must be examined. In assessing evidence for explanations, over and above the assessment of their descriptive components, we must consider whether the theoretical assumptions involved are plausible and whether the explanatory factor appealed to is the most convincing one in the case concerned. With evaluations, again we must assess the descriptive claims involved but may also need to examine the values on which they are based, their justification and application. Finally, I looked at assessment of the conclusions drawn from the findings of ethnographic studies. I considered the sorts of evidence necessary to sustain theoretical inference and empirical generalisation.

As indicated in Chapter 3, validity is only one aspect of the assessment of ethnographic research, relevance is equally important. I will discuss this in the next chapter.

Notes

1. See Arnold (1970) for a collection of articles exemplifying and discussing the use of the concept of 'subculture'. The articles in Burgess (1986) provide useful discussions of other problematic sociological concepts.
2. See Hammersley (1987b). Scarth (1987) also identifies some problems in allocating instances to Woods' types of survival strategy.
3. I am using the distinction between observers' reports and informants' accounts in a way that does not conform exactly to the more conventional distinction between observation and interviewing. In my view the latter does not capture accurately what is the most relevant methodological distinction: between the treatment of data as indicating something about the people, activities or settings observed by the researcher (observers' reports), and the use of data as a source of information about the people, activities or settings to which the data refer (informants' accounts). As should become clear, these two uses of data involve different, though overlapping, sets of validity threat.

   Much of the time this distinction corresponds to the more conventional one, but there are exceptions. For example, Parker *et al.* report that in interviews 'magistrates themselves expounded the criminal families thesis to us' (1981:91). In my terms this is an observer's report since the fact that the magistrates expounded this thesis is being used to tell us something about *them*, not about the families referred to. Indeed the researchers believe the magistrates to be mistaken in their views about 'criminal families'. Conversely, an ethnographer may treat some of what he or she hears in the course of participant observation as informants' accounts. Thus, in my study of an inner-city school I used what the teachers said to one another in the staffroom as a source of information about their behaviour in classrooms on occasions that I had not been able to observe.

4. The authors refer to 'transcription' of official proceedings. This term is ambiguous, but it seems unlikely that they used audio-recording.

5. I have, of course, examined this evidence in abstraction from the rest of Pollert's data and argument, which gives some further support to her analysis.

6. The authors actually say that because the magistrate said this we 'might wonder' if the status of the car influenced the decision. But they seem to give considerable weight to this interpretation.

7. '"Due process" is a term which means the conduct of legal proceedings according to established principles and rules which safeguard the position of the individual charged' (Walker 1980).

8. I shall concentrate on Countyside here, though the claim relates to City as well.

9. Cressey did investigate some cases where the conditions of his theory held, but not in a systematic way. For fuller discussion of these issues, see Hammersley (1989).

10. What I shall present here is a rational reconstruction of these studies: my discussion will not match perfectly or exhaust the purposes of their authors. For more extended accounts of this research, see Hammersley (1985) and Foster *et al.* (1996:ch. 4).

11. Lacey is aware of these factors and incorporates some of them into his account, but as subordinate factors to differentiation.

12. One thing that did not remain the same was the pupils, and differences between the cohorts of pupils may have affected Ball's findings. Also, the change in organisational structure itself may have had a temporary effect on attitudes.

13. There has been some additional work on this theory: see for example Quine (1974), Lacey (1974) and Abraham (1989 and 1995). Much of this has been concerned with whether setting, as well as streaming, causes polarisation.

14. The belief that statistical sampling theory is the only reasonable basis for empirical generalisation is another example of the misguided search for certainty that I criticised in Chapter 3. It is sometimes assumed that statistical techniques can provide the basis for knowing for sure whether findings are generalisable. They cannot do this. Even at best, they only tell us what are the chances of the generalisation being false.

15. As I noted in Chapter 2, ethnographers rarely distinguish between theoretical inference and empirical generalisation in a very clear way. As a result, the arguments they put forward often combine the two. In such circumstances, we must consider the validity of the conclusions both as theoretical inferences and as empirical generalisations.

CHAPTER 5

Making an assessment: relevance

I argued in Chapter 3 that it was not sufficient for the findings of an ethnographic study to be true for them to have value. Equally important is that they make a contribution to knowledge that is relevant to some public concern. In this chapter I want to discuss the nature of relevance in more detail, and to look at some of the problems and controversies involved in assessing studies in terms of this criterion.

It seems to me that there are two aspects of relevance:

1. *The importance of the topic.* The research topic must relate (however remotely) to an issue of public importance.
2. *The contribution of the conclusions to existing knowledge.* The research findings must add something to our knowledge of the issue to which they relate. Research that merely confirms what is already beyond reasonable doubt makes no contribution.

In these terms research findings may connect with an important topic but still not be relevant since they do not tell us anything new about it. For instance, research informing us that the police sometimes employ force against suspects would have little relevance, even though it concerns an important issue, because it tells us something we already know. Conversely, findings may be novel but of little relevance because they do not relate to any issue of significance. For example, the fact that in Amsterdam early one Friday afternoon in the 1970s a police van came to pick up an old man and two dogs (Punch 1979:138) may be news to most of us, in the sense that we did not know it before, but in itself it has little general importance (as far as I know) and therefore little relevance (nor does Punch claim otherwise). Importance and contribution are necessary and jointly sufficient conditions for relevance, and we must assess any set of findings in terms of both. I will look at each of them in turn.

Importance

Assessment of the relevance of ethnographic studies, and especially of the importance of the research focus, is even more open to uncertainty and disagreement than assessments of their validity. I can illustrate this, and some of the problems involved, by looking at a debate that took place over an article about muggers by Robert Lejeune. He describes a typical mugging from the mugger's point of view, drawing on interviews with 45 people who had committed one or more muggings. He identifies the salient problems facing muggers in carrying out an attack (such as controlling their own fear and ensuring the 'cooperation' of the victim), along with the strategies used to deal with these problems (Lejeune 1977). Judith Posner wrote a response to this article criticising its focus on several grounds (Posner 1980). She was not challenging the validity of the claims made; indeed she comments that the study is 'painstaking and sensitive in its depiction' (p. 104). Rather, she argues that it amounts to a kind of 'bizarre sociological voyeurism' (p. 104).[1] And she suggests that 'this study reflects a trend in ethnographic studies of deviance away from work that is relevant to 'practical problems in the real world' towards studies that are 'detached and meaningless' (p. 109). She comments that 'the study of deviance has become an end in itself, a form of sociological entertainment' (p. 109).

Posner argues that the justification for social research lies in solving either practical or conceptual problems. In terms of the first sort of problem: 'understanding the mugger's vulnerability should either help us to defend ourselves against him or to rehabilitate him after he is caught. (It could even help us catch him!)' (p. 110). However, she claims that 'Lejeune ... never attends to such matters'. Furthermore, Lejeune's article does not address a conceptual problem either: 'although he ends his article with brief allusions to vulnerability and ego, he never really ties in his research with an existing body of research on similar issues' (p. 110). Posner suggests that the research is presented as 'a mere slice of life' which 'seems to exist for its own sake' (p. 110). And she concludes that:

Sociologists, especially sociologists in the deviance area, are probably frequently motivated to research the bizarre in much the same way that anthropologists have traditionally gotten a kick out of studying far and distant peoples.

(Posner 1980:111)

Posner is here questioning the value of Lejeune's research focus, claiming that he does not relate it to any important public issue. And she uses the discussion of his article to suggest that this is a general problem with ethnographic research. The charge of voyeurism, an interest in the exotic for the personal (and

perhaps deviant!) gratification of social scientists, has been made
by others about the sociology of deviance (Liazos 1972). And
the criticism that research topics are chosen with little consideration for their public importance is also sometimes directed at
ethnographic research in other areas as well. Posner herself refers
to the study of 'conversational pausing' as a topic that might be
thought of as trivial. Ethnomethodological research, which has
included study of that topic, has often been the brunt of criticism
for being concerned with trivia.[2] More conventional ethnographic
research may also seem to be open to this charge. Take the
following examples from one of the major journals publishing
ethnographic research in sociology: 'the pet as a "family
member"' (Hickrod and Schmitt 1982), 'CB and the experience
of sex typing' (Danneker and Kasen 1981), 'amateur and professional astronomers' (Stebbins 1982). Are these not trivial
topics?

The question of the importance of research topics is certainly a
key issue that both producers and readers of ethnographic work
must consider. However, it requires careful consideration. In
Chapter 3 I pointed to the pressure for relevance to be defined in
narrow terms of immediate payoff for practical problems. I argued
there that it was essential that researchers be allowed to investigate
issues that *ought* to be problematic for practitioners but are not,
and also topics whose relevance to public issues is indirect and
perhaps quite remote (because a division of labour is necessary
within research). I also drew attention to how our sense of what
topics are important can be shaped by assumptions that are a
product of our everyday concerns and/or of the historically
produced relevances built into particular social science disciplines.
Sometimes these relevances are reasonable enough, but sometimes
they are not.

The implication of these points is that one cannot always tell at a
glance what the importance of a research topic is. It is easy to
dismiss topics as trivial simply because one does not recognise the
links that they have with more important issues, or because they do
not relate to matters that are conventionally regarded as of
significance. I can illustrate the first of these points by reference
to one of the examples mentioned earlier. While apparently trivial,
the study of pauses in conversation, along with work on other
aspects of conversational organisation, has relevance for example
both to studies of power relations in communication between
women and men and to investigations of political oratory and its
effects (Beattie 1984, Atkinson 1984, West and Zimmerman 1987).
And these seem to me to be topics of considerable importance.

That reliance on conventional views about what is important may be defective is illustrated by another of the topics referred to above: the study of 'pets as family members'. Loneliness is a major social problem in modern industrial societies, and the keeping of animal pets is a strategy used by many to cope with that problem. From this point of view, the study of pets could well be an important issue. Equally, people's attitudes towards and relationships with pets are of significance for the issue of animal rights. In some respects the pet is in a privileged situation compared to humans' treatment of other types of animal; but it may nonetheless be a situation that has unacceptable aspects (for example, the caging of birds or the castration of dogs and cats).[3] This is not to say that all of the topics that ethnographic research addresses are important, and there may well be disagreement about the examples I have discussed. The point is simply that we must reflect carefully on the importance of particular studies, rather than making snap judgements.

The case of Lejeune's study of muggers is more straightforward, I think, than the examples I have discussed above. It is not difficult to see mugging as an important public issue that ought to be addressed by research. And Lejeune's specific focus on the strategies used by muggers might well contribute to our ability to reduce the incidence of this crime, to apprehend and rehabilitate muggers; even though it does not do this directly.[4] Posner's dismissal of the importance of Lejeune's research seems to have arisen from the fact that he did not provide a rationale for it that she found convincing. This raises a particularly important issue about how we set about assessing relevance: how far we must rely on the rationales provided by authors themselves.

While the authors of ethnographic accounts usually do give some rationale for their research focus, this is not always the case. As an example, here is the opening paragraph of French and French's article on 'Gender imbalances in the primary classroom':

It is now well established that in mixed sex classrooms male pupils receive more teacher attention than do females. Brophy and Good, for example, have observed that 'boys have more interactions with the teacher than girls and appear to be generally more salient in the teacher's perceptual field' (1970, p. 373). Stanworth (1981) and Spender (1982) have also noted an imbalance in this respect and, although their formulation is more tentative, Galton, Simon and Croll's conclusion is in essence the same: 'There does appear to be a slight tendency for ... boys to receive more contact than girls' (1980, p. 66).

The present study reveals imbalances in teacher–pupil contact which, in broad terms, are compatible with these observations. However, rather than simply reporting the occurrence of the imbalances ... the principal aim of this study is to provide the basis for ... an explanation....

(French and French 1984:127)

There is a clear account here of the focus of the research, and of its relationship to other literature. However, there is no indication of why this focus is believed to be important; nor is this explained elsewhere in the article.

Whether justification for a research focus is necessary, and how much is required, are matters of judgement. There is no naturally given end point to the process of justification. However much is provided, we could in principle always ask for more. Equally, some topics may be judged to need little or no justification. For example, Lejeune provides the following rationale for his account of the strategies adopted by muggers: 'In contrast to the public indignation and journalistic concern generated by this type of street crime ..., (mugging) suffers from neglect on the part of sociologists' (Lejeune 1977:123). In my view, while this is extremely brief it is sufficient. The relationship of his research to the question of how mugging occurs and therefore to how it might be avoided and discouraged is obvious. By contrast, I do not find French and French's topic of such clear importance. (You may not agree. It would not be unreasonable to argue that discovering any substantial difference in the behaviour or treatment of girls and boys is of interest in itself; but I must ask you to bear with me for the purposes of the following discussion.) The appropriate response to a lack of what the reader believes to be sufficient justification is not to conclude (as Posner seems to do) that the study is without justification, but rather to consider whether a plausible rationale for the focus can be constructed. Here is my effort to do this for French and French's study. In this case there seem to be at least two, by no means incompatible, bases for justification:

- that an imbalance in classroom participation, or teacher attention, between boys and girls is unfair in itself;
- that this imbalance is believed to contribute significantly to differential school performance and occupational placement, and thus to differences in income, status and power between the sexes in adult life.

What is involved in constructing a rationale is to show how the research topic might contribute to our knowledge about one or more policy issues that are (and/or ought to be) of public concern. And in assessing rationales for research foci, two considerations must be borne in mind: whether the focus can be linked, however remotely, to a value many people would accept as not in need of further justification; and whether the links between the focus and that value are judged to be sound.

In the case of French and French's article, I find the first possible justification (that an imbalance in teacher attention is unfair in itself) unconvincing because I do not accept the notion of fairness to which appeal is made. Why should we insist that boys and girls in a class receive equal amounts of aggregate teacher attention? Surely we would expect teachers to take account, to one degree or another, of the individual characteristics of pupils in dealing with them: of variations in their background knowledge and their interests, their abilities and disabilities, the opportunities they have and have not had, and so on, as well as of what they do in the classroom? All of these considerations may affect the amount of attention the teacher gives them. Of course, some of these characteristics will be randomly distributed with respect to sex, so that over time and across different school classes they will not produce aggregate differences between girls and boys; though we cannot assume that they will balance one another within any single lesson, and all of French and French's data come from one lesson. However, some of these characteristics *may* be systematically related to sex. An obvious example is that on average boys may be more prone to classroom disruption than girls. If this is so, then it is reasonable to expect that teachers would give more attention (in the form of warnings and reprimands) to some proportion of the boys, both for their own good and for that of the rest of the class. Given this, it is not obvious to me that equal aggregate teacher attention between the sexes is a good thing, in a single lesson or even over a long period. Here, the suggested value criterion in terms of which the research focus is judged important is not one that I think it is reasonable to accept.

The other possible justification for French and French's research focus (that the differential distribution of teacher attention might help produce underachievement by girls in school that has consequences for their life chances) is problematic in another way. I accept the value that is appealed to here (equality of educational and occupational opportunity between the sexes). However, I have doubts about the causal link between differential teacher attention and girls' underachievement. Once again, these doubts stem in large part from the authors' focus on *amount* of teacher attention. It seems unlikely that this is strongly related to levels of educational achievement. Much more plausible would be the claim that differences in the frequency of particular types of teacher attention, such as praise and blame, might affect achievement levels. Furthermore, it has increasingly come to be recognised that, in Britain at least, girls underachieve compared to boys only in certain areas of the curriculum, notably in mathematics, physics and chemistry, and that even these differences have been reduced over the past few years (see Foster *et al.* 1996:ch. 6). Here, then, I accept the importance of the value issue to which this rationale appeals, but I have doubts about the effective relevance of the study to that value.

We can see from my discussion of French and French's study that rationales for research foci always involve value assumptions, and often factual assumptions as well. And assessing the importance of a topic requires us to make judgements about those assumptions. While disagreements about both facts and values cannot be resolved by simple demonstrations based on premises that are beyond all possible doubt, neither is outside the scope of rational argument. In both cases appeal must be made to grounds that the person advancing the argument accepts as beyond reasonable doubt and that the intended audience can reasonably be expected to accept in the same way. One of my criticisms of French and French's paper is that they assume that the justification for their focus is obvious and sound, whereas in my view it is problematic. But, of course, in assessing the rationale for this study, I have taken the value of equal educational and occupational opportunites for men and women to be beyond doubt: not only do I accept it but I have assumed that you as reader do too, so that there is no need for me to provide justificatory argument in support of it. But I could be wrong about this. There are religious and political views that reject this value, arguing for example that women and men are suited to different spheres of life. As already noted, the process of justification is potentially endless; and all we can do is to stop the argument where it seems reasonably unlikely that dispute will occur (and take it up again if we are proven wrong). It is essential to recognise, though, that what is at issue here is not a decision about what are the most important research topics, but simply whether particular studies relate to a topic that has importance.

While I believe that Posner's assessment of Lejeune's study is largely misconceived because it ignores the justification for that study's focus which can be constructed relatively easily and convincingly, I think her argument does raise an important issue about the coordination of ethnographic studies. Even where studies do explicitly relate their research focus to public issues, they rarely seem to be coordinated with one another well enough to deal with those issues. It is not enough for studies to be loosely related to matters of public concern; they should be collectively organised to address those matters. And this coordination is weak at best in many areas. This leads us into discussion of the other aspect of arguments about relevance: the question of the distinctive contribution that particular studies make.

Contribution

Besides assessing whether the focus of a study is important we must also judge the contribution it makes to what we already know, and this involves looking at its relationship to other studies that are available, and to commonsense knowledge. As I noted earlier, a study's findings might be important but contribute little because they are already well-established through research and/or merely confirm what we already take to be beyond reasonable doubt on the basis of everyday experience.[5]

An example of criticism of research for failing to make a contribution to our knowledge can be found in some comments on a study of 'patter merchants', market traders who engage in an elaborate 'spiel' which attracts an audience and persuades some of its members to buy the goods on offer (Pinch and Clark 1986, Cherrington *et al.* 1987). Pinch and Clark examine the structure of such 'spiels', using conversation analysis to show how their structure is designed to achieve mass sales: for example through the use of contrasts that highlight the supposed value and low price of what is for sale. Cherrington *et al.* accept that the operation of local markets is an important sociological topic, but they deny that Pinch and Clark tell us anything new about this topic:

> Our impression is that, crucially, much of the analysis consists of a description of the sales pitch which is rather obvious to most people who have ever bought goods in an English market. ... That market pitchers use talk and non-verbal communication to try to persuade people to buy goods which they might not actually want, and have a measure of success in doing this, should come as no great revelation to anyone. Whilst this lack of anything other than 'common-sense' description struck us most forcibly, Pinch and Clark clearly believe that they are describing something which we could not have known without their research, and that the results are important, even revelatory. We can only conclude that the authors' naive fascination with the 'accomplishment' of the pitchers' talk led them to minimise the importance of the social interaction, to the detriment of the seriousness and relevance of their sociology.
>
> (Cherrington *et al.* 1987:278–9)[6]

In making an assessment of criticisms such as these, we must consider the various ways in which studies may contribute to existing knowledge. It is perhaps worth emphasising, first, that the idea of 'contribution' does not deny the value of all studies that confirm previous findings. I argued in Chapter 3 that within the research community the level of routine scepticism about what is known should be higher than outside, that it should be determined by the common ground among researchers of different political views, practical interests and background experience; this scepticism being designed to minimise the chances of accepting as true what is in fact false. Given this, there is considerable scope for research designed to check the findings of previous studies, especially where this involves triangulation: the use of sources of information likely to involve different types and directions of validity threat compared to the original study. Thus, one sort of contribution that research can make is to test previous findings and put them beyond reasonable doubt. And, indeed, in my view this is a function to which too little research is directed.

Perhaps the most common contribution claimed for ethnographic studies, however, is that they fill a gap in the literature, in the sense of dealing with a phenomenon about which there has been little previous research. As we saw, this was the rationale that Lejeune provided for his study of mugging, and Pinch and Clark adopt the same justification. They open their article by claiming that 'There is no body of research which has systematically examined the interactional skills and processes involved in selling...' (Pinch and Clark 1986:169).

The principle behind this sort of rationale is developed by Howard Becker in his discussion of the Chicago School studies of the 1920s and 1930s. He argues that these formed part of a mosaic that offered a picture of Chicago social life as it was at that time (Becker 1966). While subsequent studies have not been so geographically specific, the same sort of rationale applies in the sense that they may give us a picture of the various categories of actor and situation making up modern societies. Thus, we have studies telling us about the perspectives and practices of police officers and tramps, prostitutes and doctors, journalists and drug dealers and so on, and of the settings and institutions in which they are involved.

It should be noted, however, that this rationale involves a problematic element of empirical generalisation. There is heterogeneity as well as homogeneity among such categories of actor and institution.[7] And this indicates another important way in which ethnographic studies can complement one another. Studies may contribute to the literature by providing information about other cases in a population that previous studies have sought to generalise about on the basis of too small or too homogeneous a sample. As we saw in Chapter 4, ethnographic studies frequently claim that the cases they studied are typical, so that generalisation to some larger population can be made, but that often this is not well-established. And we noted there how other studies, especially of cases strategically selected to contrast with those investigated previously, would allow much more convincing generalisation and also document the sorts of heterogeneity to be found within the population. You may remember that it was in these terms that Punch justified his study of policing in the *Warmoesstraat* district of Amsterdam: that there had been a relative neglect of policing in the inner city by researchers and that his study would thereby extend the empirical basis for generalisations about police work (Punch 1979).

Such plugging of gaps in our current knowledge, whether in the form of studies in previously neglected areas or of research that widens the basis for sound generalisation, is not the only way in which the findings of ethnographic accounts can make an important contribution. They may also serve to challenge and reformulate what were previously taken to be facts, whether on the basis of everyday experience or of previous studies. A striking example is to be found in research on 'soccer hooliganism' where findings are often contrasted with defective commonsense and media understandings of the phenomenon. Peter Marsh, for example, tries to show that contrary to the widespread assumption that the behaviour of football fans is disorderly, it is ritually structured and highly predictable, and therefore less dangerous for participants and bystanders than might appear (Marsh *et al.* 1978). Dunning *et al.*, dealing with the same topic, argue that contrary to popular belief hooliganism has accompanied association football ever since its establishment in the 1870s and 1880s, and that it is not a fashion that will lapse in due course but a way of life for those engaged in it (Dunning *et al.* 1988). Clearly, such revision of what was previously accepted as knowledge can be of great value (assuming, of course, that the new knowledge is itself valid).

Equally, studies may be concerned with checking whether previously established facts are still true. Here the interest is in the extent and character of social change. The most obvious illustrations of this are community restudies. For example the primary motivation of the Lynds in restudying Middletown was to discover how life there had changed as a result of the Depression (Lynd and Lynd 1937). Similarly, in studying Plainville the Gallahers took the information provided by West's original study as a base-line from which to chart the changes that had occurred in the town during the intervening 15 years (Gallaher 1964). The same sort of motivation sometimes underlies studies of different cases of the same category of phenomena at different times. Thus, Ball was concerned with whether the same processes of differentiation and polarisation discovered under the selective education system by Hargreaves and Lacey would also be found in schools after comprehensive reform (Hargreaves 1967, Lacey 1970, Ball 1981, see also Abraham 1989 and 1995).

Finally, studies may be related to one another in that they contribute to the development and testing of the same theory. The studies by Hargreaves, Lacey, Ball and Abraham make a contribution in this way too (a fact which illustrates that accounts may make more than one type of contribution to our knowledge). As we saw in the previous chapter, these studies develop and test differentiation-polarisation theory in settings that both vary the level of differentiation and control some of the other relevant variables. In this way they complement one another in a manner that few other ethnographic studies have done (Hammersley 1985).

It is in terms of these sorts of relationship between the findings of a study and existing knowledge that we need to assess the contribution made by those findings. Studies are not always explicit about the contribution they are intended to make, and are often not directed towards other literature in such a way that they produce a cumulation of knowledge in any very clear and effective manner. There is a strong tendency for ethnographic accounts to be produced so as, in large part, to stand alone, having only weak relationships to other studies. This is encouraged by the conceptualisation of their goal in terms of theoretical description, whereby great emphasis is placed on the particular case(s) studied. Just as many anthropologists in the past conceived of themselves as producing knowledge about their chosen tribe, so ethnographic sociologists often seem to view themselves as simply describing a setting for its own sake. While they recognise that general conclusions must be drawn, the relationship between these and those of other studies is often not very strong. Another factor is an excessive emphasis on novelty. A result of this is that much more ethnographic research is concerned with opening up new areas or generating new analytical approaches than is devoted to systematically building on what has been done before.

In my view we need to move to a situation where there is less emphasis on the investigation of new phenomena or the generation of new ideas (important as these are) and more on improving existing knowledge, whether empirical, theoretical, or methodological. This will require that the links among studies be made more explicit and stronger, so that the contribution of past research and the priorities for future research become clearer.

Conclusion

In this chapter I have looked at two components of relevance: the importance of the topic and the contribution of the findings. And I have discussed some of the difficulties and disagreements involved in their application. As with the assessment of validity, assessment of the relevance of a study is a matter of judgement; and, even more obviously than in the case of validity, it can involve disagreement. There is no simple answer or easy route to consensus. But that does not mean that we cannot make rational judgements about the relevance of ethnographic research; or that we should not seek consensus. In the next chapter I will present a detailed discussion of one of my own articles to provide a more extended illustration of what is involved in assessing the validity and relevance of an ethnographic account.

Notes

1. She also questions its ethics: whether its publication was likely to have unacceptable consequences. I shall discuss this issue in Chapter 7. There are several published replies to Posner: Lejeune (1980), Sagarin (1980) and Cohen (1980).
2. See McNall and Johnson (1975) for an example. For an ethnomethodological reply to this criticism, see Sharrock and Anderson (1986).
3. Interestingly, while the article referred to here touches on both these issues, neither is its main focus: it uses the family pet as a case for developing and testing Goffman's frame analysis (Hickrod and Schmitt 1982). In Posner's terms it addresses a conceptual problem.
4. Lejeune had also studied *victims* of mugging. His interest in the topic was stimulated by being mugged himself.
5. There is a trade-off between plausibility and contribution. The more plausible are findings, the less of a contribution they will make; and the more of a contribution they make, the less likely they can be accepted as plausible at face value.
6. For Pinch and Clark's reply to these charges. see Pinch and Clark (1987).
7. This problem arises with the Chicago studies too. Becker notes that Chicagoans tended to view Chicago as typical of other cities, though they rarely addressed this issue explicitly.

CHAPTER 6

An example

In previous chapters I have outlined the principles which I believe ought to guide the reading and assessment of ethnographic studies. In this chapter I provide an example of a sustained assessment of a particular article and thereby, in what I hope is the most useful way, exemplify the application of the principles I have advocated. The article I will assess is reprinted in the Appendix to this book. It is an account of the functions of the talk among teachers in a secondary school staffroom. I wrote it on the basis of ethnographic fieldwork in a school I called 'Downtown', carried out in the early 1970s.

Assessing one's own research is as important as assessing anyone else's. However, in doing so one is in both a more and a less privileged position than other readers: one knows more of the background, but is perhaps not able to attain the same critical distance. You will have to judge how far (and how legitimately) I have made use of the advantage and how well I have overcome the disadvantage. Indeed, you might wish to carry out your own assessment of the article before you read mine.

I will begin by providing a summary of the argument, using the framework suggested in Chapter 2. Then I will assess the validity of the claims made and the relevance of the research focus.

Summary

The focus of the study was social interaction in school staffrooms, and the information we can gain from this about the structure of social relationships among teachers. However, the more specific topic is the exchange of 'news' about pupils among teachers, the aim being to describe and explain the features of this news exchange. Only a very brief rationale is presented: appealing to previous neglect of the general focus, and its significance for the sociology of occupations and for explaining teachers' behaviour in classrooms.

The case studied is the staffroom in a 'small, inner-city, boys' secondary modern school'. No further information about the school is provided in this article, though more can be found in a research biography published elsewhere, and in the Ph.D. thesis from which the article derives (Hammersley 1984, Hammersley 1980). The thesis tells us much about the school's local context, internal organisation and history. It was located within an inner-city area of a large northern conurbation which was occupied by many Asian and 'West Indian' families, as well as by some white 'problem' families. In the past the building had been an elementary school, but after it became a secondary modern in the early 1950s it was one of the few such schools to have a GCE examination stream. As a result, it had attracted pupils from outside its catchment area. In more recent years, however, this inflow of pupils had stopped as a result of the opening of a new school nearby. The number of pupils had also dropped to around 300, half of what it had been; and pupils were no longer entered for GCE at 16 + . Many of the teachers at the school had taught there for several years, witnessing what they regarded as a sharp decline in the quality of the pupils.

No information is given about research methods in the article, though we can assume participant observation in the staffroom was involved (in what role is not clear). Again, further information is available in the other sources. Most of the data were gathered by the researcher sitting in the staffroom and participating in or overhearing conversations among the teachers. Some also arose from conversations between teachers and the researcher on the way to or from classrooms or staffroom (and in the strict sense was therefore not staffroom talk). The fieldwork took place over a period of two terms, the researcher spending three days a week in the school, on average. The researcher was much younger than most of the teachers, and was regarded as inexperienced by them, being treated in many respects like the students on teaching practice who were present in the school for much of the fieldwork period. The data were fieldnotes based on jotted notes made on the spot and, written up in the evenings. The researcher was not a teacher in the school, and his role as researcher was overt. However, the teachers did not know that he was taking notes about what they said in the staffroom.

The major claims made in the article consist of both description and explanation of the staffroom talk. There are three main descriptive claims. First, there is the identification of four types of staffroom news, dealing with:

● specific events,
● the moods of particular classes,

- the presence or absence of 'trouble-makers',
- summary typifications of troublesome pupils.

These are supported by extracts from fieldnotes instancing each type.

Second, there is the claim that staffroom news is preoccupied with threats to classroom order. The fieldnote extracts illustrating the types of news are intended to support this claim too. There is also an examination of exceptions to this generalisation: news items dealing with pupils' ability.

Third, it is claimed that underlying staffroom talk at Downtown there is a standard set of pupil types, consisting of: the 'unstable', the 'louts', the 'easily led', and the 'immature'. It is also noted that the teachers recognised that pupils sometimes moved between these types over time. Each of these pupil typifications is illustrated with fieldnote extracts, as are teachers' discussions of changes in the character of individual pupils.

There seem to be two main explanatory claims:

1. That staffroom news is exchanged at Downtown because it provides information that teachers find useful given their work circumstances: they work in separate classrooms but recurrently face the same pupils. Little or no evidence is provided for this over and above that presented in support of the descriptive claims.
2. That staffroom news is not just a matter of information exchange but is also 'rhetorical'. It involves accounting for pupils' indiscipline in such a way as to deflect blame for it away from the teachers and from the approach to teaching to which they are committed. This is done by 'cutting out' the contexts of pupil behaviour described, thereby presenting it as purely a product of pupil character. Additional fieldnote extracts are provided and analysed to show that their structure is compatible with this interpretation, and two published sources are also drawn on.

There are no conclusions in the article that explicitly go beyond the case. However, these must be implied given the nature of the stated research focus. I think we must assume that the author intended the main claims about Downtown either to provide the basis for empirical generalisation to other staffrooms (though to what population of these is unclear) or to relate to some theoretical inference about the functions of staffroom talk. It is difficult to be more specific than this (even for me!).

Validity

Definitions

There are a couple of minor definitional issues. First, there is the use of the (much-abused) term 'rhetorical'. Strictly speaking, 'rhetoric' refers simply to the stylistic strategies used to persuade audiences. In addition, there is a derogatory usage, indicating something that is persuasively presented but unsound; and something like this is presumably intended here. The implication is that the function of staffroom talk is not merely referential (as it needs to be for exchanging information). Rather, it is designed to reinforce certain already held assumptions on the part of the speaker (and others) and thereby to provide mutual reassurance. It might be clearer to refer to this as the reassurance or reinforcement (rather than the rhetorical) function of staffroom talk. In any event, the sense of the term 'rhetorical' is not entirely clear and a definition would have been useful.

The other issue concerns the 'cutting out' of context. All descriptions cut out some parts of the context of the events described, and include others. What is argued here, in effect, is that contextual features which the author regards as important for explaining pupils' behaviour are omitted from staffroom talk at Downtown. While the author's judgement about this matter may be reasonable, it is important to recognise that this is the basis for identifying where context has been left out. A definition of the *sort* of cutting out of context being claimed would have clarified matters.

Descriptive claims

I do not believe that we can accept any of these claims at face value as sufficiently plausible; and their credibility probably does require support with evidence, which the author provides. There are a number of questions that we must ask about this evidence, however. First, we need to consider the possible effects of reactivity. While data collection in the staffroom was effectively covert, the researcher's identity as researcher was known, and so we cannot rule out even procedural reactivity. Personal reactivity is clearly also a possibility; though the fact that the researcher seems to have been regarded as low status by the teachers suggests that his presence may not have led them to hide their views and actions. And the data themselves suggest that much which might have been hidden was not. The fact that the researcher was in the field for a lengthy and fairly intensive period of time would also reduce the danger of the teachers maintaining a front for the researcher, since fronts are difficult to sustain over long periods. On balance, the risk that reactivity has seriously distorted the data seems low.[1]

Second, we must ask how accurately what the teachers said was recorded. Since the data were fieldnotes, not transcriptions of audio recordings, this perhaps indicates some inaccuracy. And the fact that observation in the staffroom was covert added to the problem, as the author indicates in the research biography:

Noting down what was said on the spot was very difficult, being done in a surreptitious and hurried manner. On one occasion I was forced to jot down notes on the newspaper I was reading, hoping that no-one would ask to borrow it. There had been comments ... about my reading a 'liberal' newspaper like *The Guardian* and on that basis I hoped I was safe! Often jotted notes had to be made after I had left the staffroom. While I tried to note down literally what was said, I may have made mistakes. While I can claim that even where I did not get the words exactly right I probably got the sense of what was said, that unfortunately builds in a reliance on the interpretation of sense I made on the spot. Also important here is the relevance of context. I often wonder now in reading these data whether anything was said before or after the recorded exchange which would modify interpretation of it. Once again there is reliance here on my on-the-spot decisions. Even more important, it is possible that on some occasions, rather than simply not remembering the exact words used, I may have forgotten whole sentences or stretches of conversation which came between one utterance and the next in the recorded exchange.

(Hammersley 1984:53–4)

Obviously, this does raise a serious threat to validity. What is especially important to consider is whether any systematic bias seems likely to have been operating (perhaps unconsciously) on the researcher's data recording. For example, his political views about the authoritarian character of traditional teaching (which are revealed in the research biography) may have led him to misinterpret comments in such a way that they confirmed his expectations. On balance, though, it seems unlikely that the validity of the account would be wholly undermined by these problems.

Another issue concerns generalisability within the case: how far is the staffroom talk of the whole staff during the relevant period captured accurately? Out of a total of 19 teachers, 13 are quoted in the article, but some much more frequently than others. In his research biography the author notes that he had much closer contact with some teachers than with others. Might his account of staffroom culture at Downtown have been biased by this differential contact? In my judgement, this seems relatively unlikely, given the degree of coverage of the staff and the fact that many of the comments recorded were made in public, often involving collaboration among multiple speakers, and most of the time without any apparent signs of disagreement. Similarly, while we are not told from what stage of the fieldwork the various quotes come, there seems no obvious reason to suppose that they are likely to be unrepresentative of the whole.[2]

However, while this may be true in general terms, we could still raise questions about the representativeness of the data used to support particular claims. For example, was it really the case that the teachers used a standard set of four pupil types? Even on the basis of the data supplied, it seems unlikely that there was stability, either over time or across all the teachers. Indeed, the terms used to refer to the pupils in the extracts quoted in the article are much more diverse than this, and include at least one that does not match the typology, namely 'good lad' (Extract 14).

Another question concerns the relationship between what was recorded in the fieldnotes and what actually occurred in the Downtown staffroom during the period of the fieldwork. Here again selective bias may have been operating on the part of the researcher, perhaps reflecting his political prejudices, and we have no basis for checking this.

Finally, we must consider the relationship between the data extracts and the claims they are intended to support. In my judgement this relationship is generally strong; there are no obviously defective interpretations.

Explanatory claims

Of course the validity of the explanatory claims depends, in part, on that of the descriptive claims discussed above. For the purposes of the assessment here I will assume that the descriptions are for the most part valid.

The first explanatory claim seems plausible. There is little description of the circumstances in which these teachers work in the article, but the claim that they operate in separate classrooms and teach many of the same pupils can be accepted as plausible and credible at face value, I believe. Furthermore, the character of the news exchanged is compatible with this explanation. And the implicit theoretical idea (that in such circumstances teachers will seek and be influenced by information about particular pupils drawn from colleagues) seems reasonable; there are no more plausible alternative explanations for the character of the staff-room talk.

The second explanatory claim, by contrast, is problematic. While reading off the motivation of staffroom comments from their content seems reasonably convincing in the case of the first claim, here it is less so. The author provides evidence to try to establish that the nature of staffroom talk is compatible with the idea that it serves a function of reassurance or reinforcement, as well as information exchange. Crucial here is the way that the accounts of pupils' behaviour exchanged by the teachers cut out the social context surrounding that behaviour, and especially the teachers' own actions. And, indeed, it does seem that all the extracts quoted in the article have this feature.[3] Of course, we do not know whether those quoted are representative of the corpus of data collected, though we can check this against the complete set of data presented in the thesis (and we find, I think, that they are representative in this respect). More difficult to assess is whether these data are representative of staffroom news exchanged at Downtown in the relevant period. There is no way of checking this, but I think we can take the data quoted as indicating a tendency for staffroom news at Downtown to have this character. There is, of course, little description of the explanatory factor itself: the teachers' need for reassurance. It is simply claimed that the Downtown teachers find the failure of the pupils to live up to their expectations threatening. Perhaps, though, we can accept this as sufficiently plausible at face value, and there is some evidence in the thesis to support it.

The theoretical assumption involved in this explanation (that, faced with failure teachers committed to a traditional conception of teaching will blame either themselves or the pupils and/or parents), also seems plausible. There is, however, at least one other reasonable explanation for the way in which staffroom news excluded the social context of the event described: that the teachers simply believed (perhaps rightly) that psychological factors were the most important ones causing pupils' behaviour. The author does not address this issue; he avoids it in large part by the sleight of hand involved in using 'cutting out context' to refer to cutting out references to the role of the teacher. He trades on the fact that no-one could reasonably deny the relevance of context to explanations. Explanations necessarily appeal to *some* contextual feature as the causal factor. The specific relevance of the role of the teacher, on the other hand, needs to be argued for, but no such argument is provided.[4] The implicit argument that the author adopts is that since the staff's explanations do not properly explain, they can be no more than excuses. But given that the premiss of this argument has not been established, we should not accept the conclusion. And, on top of this, the logic of the argument itself is questionable. There is no reason to assume that because an explanation is false its communication must have been intended to serve some other function than that of providing true information (any more than we should assume that the communication of a true explanation cannot be intended to serve some other function than information exchange). All this is not to reject the explanation offered, simply to point out that there are some serious problems in establishing it which are not addressed in this article or in the other sources.

Conclusions

As I noted earlier, there are no conclusions presented in the article. The discussion under the heading of 'Conclusion' simply summarises the main claims. However, given the declared focus of the research, we must assume that some broader conclusions are implied. And since it is not made clear whether what is intended is theoretical inference or empirical generalisation, we must consider the possibility of each. It should be said, though, that neither looks promising.

If what is intended is empirical generalisation, we must ask: to what population is it believed that the findings should be generalisable? The focus seems to relate to all schools. Yet, even putting aside the illegitimacy of such unrestricted generalisation, it seems most unlikely that many of the features of this school would be generalisable even to other secondary schools in England and Wales in the 1970s. The fact that it was a secondary modern, that it was single sex, and its small size were all atypical features even at that time; and these probably have consequences which make the case atypical in other respects too. It may be that the school is typical of small, boys' inner-city secondary moderns in the early 1970s, but the author does not tell us why we should be interested in this population. Furthermore, there is no evidence supplied even for this generalisation.

Justifying inference from case to focus on the basis of theoretical inference is perhaps more promising. There are theoretical ideas in the account, notably concerning the functions of staffroom talk. However, these seem to be used as a basis for explaining the features found in the Downtown staffroom, rather than being put forward as theoretical ideas that have been tested in this case. For the latter to be convincing, we would need to be told why the case of Downtown is especially appropriate for a test of these ideas. No such rationale is provided. One might argue that Downtown was a situation in which teachers were subjected to maximum threat to their identities as competent practitioners (and something like this is hinted at in the thesis); but we need more clarification of the theory and of the relationship of the case to it before we can come to any reasonable judgement about the soundness of the theoretical inference involved.

Relevance

If the conclusions of this article were to be interpreted as limited to Downtown school itself, the relevance of the study would be very low. Few people would be interested in what happened in a single, pseudonymous school in the early 1970s (especially one which closed down soon after the research was completed). On this basis, while the research could be deemed to make a contribution (in the limited sense in which I have used that term in this book), the information it provides must be judged to be of little or no importance.

If wider conclusions are assumed, we must consider what their relevance might be. Here, the brief rationale provided serves some purpose. It is fairly clear, I think, that what teachers say in the staffroom may tell us a good deal about staff relationships, and that the nature of those relationships is of considerable importance for many aspects of schooling, including the effects on teachers' typifications of pupils. Furthermore, it is true that there had been little or no previous research in this area, so that research of this kind would make a useful contribution (though as I made clear in Chapter 5, in my view this is the weakest form of contribution). Unfortunately, though, the value of these general conclusions is largely undermined by the absence of evidence supporting them.

Conclusion

In summary, then, most of the descriptive claims and the first of the explanatory claims are established reasonably convincingly: the Downtown teachers do seem to have engaged in the exchange of news (of the four types specified) concerned primarily with threats to classroom order; and this does seem likely to have arisen from the character of their working conditions, that they worked separately but faced many of the same pupils. The other, and more important, explanatory claim (that news exchange also served the purpose of reinforcing the teachers' existing assumptions about the pupils and about teaching) is less well-established. While the data seem to fit it, and the theoretical assumption on which it is based is reasonable, there are problems with the author's attempt to establish the priority of this explanation. This is because he relies on drawing conclusions about the function of staffroom comments from the judgement (itself unsubstantiated) that the explanations which they contain are inadequate. An even more serious problem with this article is that it provides no basis for drawing more general conclusions from the evidence about this case. Moreover, while restricting the conclusions to the claims made about Downtown would avoid this problem, it would give the findings little or no relevance.

All this does not imply that the article is valueless. Its focus is of fairly clear relevance, and it may offer useful comparative data and theoretical ideas for subsequent studies. However, I think that we must conclude that its value is rather limited.

In this chapter I have looked at how the approach I outlined in earlier chapters might be applied to the assessment of a whole article. In the final chapter I will look at how this sort of assessment relates to some other concerns we may have in reading ethnographic studies.

Notes

1. We should be a little careful here, however. Punch (1979:13) reports that he only discovered by chance, at a party long after the fieldwork, how much the police officers he studied had hidden from him.
2. There is a brief discussion of this issue in the research biography (Hammersley 1984:52–3). Also, the thesis includes all the data that were recorded in the staffroom during the fieldwork, and the date of collection of each data item is indicated there.
3. Extract 1 may seem to be an exception, but it is not. Information about the incident to which Greaves was responding is elicited by 'What had he (the pupil) done?', and his reply concentrates entirely on the character of the pupil.
4. Ironically, I refer to this point in Note 9 in criticising others; but proceed to make the same mistake myself.

CHAPTER 7

Conclusion: varieties of assessment

As I noted at the beginning of this book, the reading of ethnographic accounts has been given much less attention than it deserves. More significantly, the issue of the standards by which such accounts should be assessed raises fundamental issues about the nature of ethnography, on which there is little consensus. The approach I have taken is not, therefore, one that all ethnographers would accept. I have sought to steer a path between, on the one hand, those views of ethnographic methodology that are based on a naive realism whereby the goal is simply to represent social phenomena 'in their own terms', and on the other hand those that abandon realism in favour of an emphasis on direct practical payoff and/or on the constructionist creativity of ethnographic analysis and writing. In doing so I advocated what I called a 'subtle realism' in which the goal is still to represent reality, but in a way that is relevant to particular purposes, and with a recognition that even claims about validity, and especially those about relevance, can only be judged on the basis of assumptions whose own validity we can never know for certain. Along with this, I have argued for the distinctive character and role of the research community, both in adopting a higher level of routine scepticism and a stronger commitment to resolving disagreement by debate than is found elsewhere, and in operating a division of labour that enables us to achieve knowledge that would not otherwise be available. Much of the book has been concerned with spelling out and illustrating the implications of this point of view for our reading of ethnographic texts.

The sort of assessment that I have been concerned with, while very important, is not the only kind. My primary concern has been with how, as researchers and students, we should read ethnographic accounts with a view to deciding whether they make a valuable contribution to our knowledge. While this probably shares much with other sorts of assessment, it does not exhaust the relevant issues. In this final chapter I will consider briefly some other sorts of assessment: that carried out by practitioners; that concerned with the competence of the researcher; and that dealing with the effectiveness and/or ethics of particular research strategies.

Practical assessment

One sort of assessment that is obviously important, given my argument that research must have some ultimate relevance for other forms of practice, is practitioners' assessments of the value of research findings. It is worth distinguishing here between two sorts of use that practitioners may make of research (there are no doubt others): first, it may be employed to satisfy a need for information that is important to their work; second, it may be used to convince others of something in order to persuade them to adopt a particular, desirable policy.

In the first situation, practitioners are likely to use the same two criteria of assessment that I outlined in earlier chapters. However, their interpretation of what is valid and relevant will probably be different from that of researchers. It is sometimes suggested that for practical purposes we require a lower level of likely validity than is usually demanded by researchers. But while I have argued that researchers should operate at a higher level of routine doubt than others, this does not mean that in all circumstances the validity requirements of practitioners will be lower than those of researchers. Indeed, in some circumstances they may be higher. Practitioners' judgements will vary from those of researchers because their experience, and thus what they find plausible, differs. Also, the threshold of validity applied may well depend on what are taken to be the implications of the claims involved, and how significant these implications are judged to be. For example, where the information implies no change of current practice, the threshold in terms of which information is judged valid may be relatively low. But where the information implies the need for fundamental change the threshold applied may be much higher. And in many circumstances this will be a reasonable approach. Similarly, where the costs of error are likely to be high, great care will usually be taken to assess validity, but where those costs are low less care may be deployed. Furthermore, we must remember that different types of practitioner are likely to vary considerably in judgements about the validity of particular claims, because of the varying salience of that claim for their concerns and because of differing experience and background assumptions.

Variation between researchers and practitioners, and among practitioner groups, occurs even more obviously in relation to the criterion of relevance. Practitioners are likely to place great value on information that is directly relevant to the problems, chronic and acute, that they face. Ideally, what they want is information that goes a long way towards solving those problems and which is available in a user-friendly form at the time when it is needed. By contrast, for the most part, they are likely to be less interested in, and less likely to see the value of, information that relates only remotely, if at all, to their problems; especially if it is information that in their terms is already well known (even if not well established from the point of view of researchers).

The other sort of value that research can have for practitioners is as a rhetorical resource in arguing the case for particular policies. Here the authority of research is used, and sometimes abused, for instrumental purposes. In this case, research findings are likely to be judged in terms of whether they support what the individual or group is seeking to promote, and whether they are likely to be convincing to the target audience. This too is a legitimate role for research to play, it seems to me, even though it carries the danger that findings may be misinterpreted, presented as better established than they are, or judged wanting against standards that none could meet. It highlights the advantage that research gains from the higher threshold of scepticism researchers adopt, since it is this which gives it the authority to be used in this way. What is 'obvious' to one group of practitioners may be far from obvious to another. Research may be able to contribute to a resolution of such disagreements. This will not always be possible, however, because the necessary knowledge may not be available or easily accessible, even for researchers. Also, we must recognise that the resolution of these disagreements has to occur in a situation in which the various parties involved have much to gain and lose depending on the outcome. This, combined with the inevitable residue of uncertainty surrounding scientific findings, often makes any consensual solution to the problem unlikely. This is true even outside the realm of *social* research. So, for example, when consumer groups, farmers and the government turn to scientists to provide the necessary information to decide whether some food product should be withdrawn because of a health risk, there is only a small chance that scientists will be able to meet the situation in a way that will satisfy all sides. This is both because of the limitations of what they can offer and because of the political character of the situation. Where social research is involved, these problems are likely to be at least as serious and probably worse.

It should be clear from my account of the relationship between research and other forms of practice in Chapter 3, and from my comments here, that some clash of perspectives is to be expected between researchers and other practitioners. And, of course, this does occur. In my view, it is probably inevitable to some degree, because of the very different concerns of the two groups and the complex nature of both research and practice (see Becker 1970:ch. 7). However, the problem can be eased, I think, by recognising the differences between these two activities, and the limited but nevertheless valuable role that research can play in both of the ways I outlined. It is particularly important that research is not regarded as capable of *replacing* practical knowledge. In addition, though, I do believe that social research is currently neither sufficiently well-funded nor sufficiently well-organised to provide in full the sort of contribution to practice of which it is capable.[1]

Assessment of researchers

Sometimes assessment is concerned with the *competence* of researchers. It is perhaps worth stressing that researchers can be competent and produce false knowledge claims and unsound conclusions, and they can also make mistakes and yet still discover the truth. Their competence must be judged not so much in terms of the value of what they produce as in terms of whether, as far as we can tell, the decisions they made at various points in the research process were reasonable, in light of their goals. In addition, some account must be taken of the circumstances in which the research was carried out: the limitations on resources, the contingencies of the research process, and so on. It is often only too easy to identify the failings of particular ethnographic studies, and even to indicate strategies that could have been employed that might have improved the results. The reader is able to employ hindsight that was not available to the researcher in the course of her or his research. This is especially important in the case of ethnographic research because it employs an exploratory and developmental approach in which the initial focus of the research may be transformed, and (at the very least) will be subject to clarification, over the course of the research. Furthermore, not only are there often severe resource constraints operating on researchers, but also they face trade-offs among different gains and losses. For instance, one can usually only study a relatively *small* number of cases *in depth*, so that often one must choose between being able to establish the generalisability of one's findings effectively or having detailed (and perhaps more accurate) information about each case.

Similarly, if one makes heavy use of the accounts of informants one can cover more ground more rapidly than if one relies on participant observation; on the other hand, the use of informants adds new potential sources of error to the data. These are not either/or matters of course, many levels of trade-off are possible; but it is not always clear what the optimum level is, and our judgement about that may change over time as the research evolves.

What all this points to is that research is itself a form of practice, and what I said about the nature of practice in Chapter 5 applies just as much here as elsewhere. In particular, we must resist the temptation to see methodology as specifying a set of rules that can simply be applied in doing research. At best, it can only provide general guidance and there is much room for disagreement about what one can and cannot, should and should not, do on any particular occasion. Assessments of the research process where what is at issue is the competence of the researcher must take account of this. What I have focused on in this book is the judgement of ethnographic accounts against ideals. Important as that is, it cannot serve alone as a basis for fair assessments of researcher competence.

Assessing the effectiveness of research strategies

Another purpose that may motivate assessment is concern with the effectiveness of the research strategies employed in a study, with a view to judging the advantages and disadvantages of these strategies for future use. Whereas quantitative researchers have long been concerned with the development and assessment of particular research techniques, for example particular types of attitude scale or modes of statistical analysis, ethnographers have shown less interest in this. In part this stems from the less structured character of ethnographic research: with its explicit concern to adapt to the circumstances being studied so as to minimise the researcher's effect, and to modify the strategies employed in accordance with the developing research problem. From these points of view there is a sense in which all aspects of a piece of ethnographic research must be unique. However, this does not mean that we cannot identify common strategies employed by ethnographers, and make some assessment of them; but we must remember the practical character and contextual variability of ethnographic research and the resulting limitation on the contribution of methodology to it.

There is now a considerable prescriptive literature about ethnographic method, and this has come to be supplemented (as I have

noted several times in this book) by research biographies.[2] Both
types of literature involve informal assessments of particular
research strategies drawing explicitly, and even more often
implicitly, on the experience of the author and of other ethnographers. However, there has been rather little formal, collective
assessment of strategies, building in a coordinated way on analysis
of the studies in which they have been used. An embryonic
example of this sort of assessment can be found in Stephen Ball's
biography of his research on Beachside Comprehensive School,
where he examines the technique of respondent validation in the
light of his own experience, and the published account by Bloor of
his use of it in studying ENT specialists (Ball 1984, Bloor 1978).
However, such assessments do not always go very far or draw on
the full range of literature available.

In making assessments of the effectiveness of particular strategies the likely validity of the research findings is an important
consideration, but it is not the only one. A technique may be
judged useful even though the findings of the studies in which it
was used are not convincing, since that failure may arise from
other factors. Conversely, even when the findings are convincing
we may conclude that the research strategy is unlikely to be very
effective in other circumstances.

Ethics

An especially important dimension of the assessment of ethnographic research concerns ethics. We may sometimes need to look
at the techniques used in ethnographic research in terms of whether
or not their use was legitimate, and there have been many disputes
about the ethics of particular ethnographic studies.[3] These have
tended to revolve around four issues: deception, privacy, damaging
effects on the people studied, and consequences for future research.

Deception

This problem arises most strikingly in the case of covert research,
where an ethnographer carries out an investigation without most
or all of the other participants being aware that research is taking
place. Examples are Roy's research on workers in a machine shop
and Homan's work on old time Pentecostalists (Roy 1952 and
1955, Homan 1978).[4]

While the issue of deception is raised most sharply by covert
research, it always arises to one degree or another. Ethnographers

rarely tell the people they are studying *everything* about the research, partly because most people are unlikely to want to know all the details, but also because of the danger that divulging information will affect their behaviour in ways that will invalidate the research. For instance, to tell teachers that one is interested in whether they normally talk as much to girls as to boys in the classroom may produce false results since they may make an effort to talk equally to both.[5] Roth has argued that all research falls on a continuum between the completely open and the completely covert (Roth 1962); and it is worth emphasising that within the same piece of research the degree of openness may vary considerably among the various people in the field and over time.

Privacy

In everyday life we draw distinctions between public places (such as streetcorners) and private places (like the bedroom), as well as between information that is intended for public consumption and that which is not. A frequent concern about ethnographic research is that it involves making public things said and done in private. Like deception, however, the concept of privacy is complex. What is public and what private is rarely clear-cut. Is the talk among people in a bar public or private, for example? We also seem to draw distinctions depending on who is involved. For instance, it is quite common for educational researchers to ask children about their friends, but it is very rare for them to investigate friendship patterns among teachers; in part, I think this stems from the assumption that children's private lives are open to scrutiny in a way that those of adults, especially professional, middle-class adults, are not. Also, privacy seems to be defined in terms of specific audiences that are and are not regarded as having legitimate access to information of particular kinds. (Not in front of the children, or not in front of the adults!) Sometimes, the invasion of privacy by researchers is justified on the grounds that since the account will be published for a specialised audience neither the people studied nor anyone else who knows them is likely to read it. But is this true? And, even if it is, does it excuse the invasion of privacy?

Social scientists have taken up contrasting positions about privacy and research. On the one hand there are those who argue that the data an ethnographer collects about a person, especially interview data, belong to that person, so that before they can be quoted in a research report permission for such quotation must be obtained.[6] At the other extreme there are those espousing what is sometimes called 'conflict methodology', who argue that researchers have a right, indeed an obligation, to investigate and to publish what they discover, especially when the subject of the research is people who are publicly accountable, or who ought to be (Rainwater and Pitman 1967, Lehman and Young 1974, Douglas 1976, Lundman and McFarlane 1976).

Damaging consequences

While ethnographic research does not usually involve the sort of damaging consequences that may be involved in, say, medical experiments, it can have consequences for the people studied, and for others. For example, publication of an ethnographic account may harm the reputations of individuals, groups or whole categories of people. A well-known example is the account of Springdale, a community in upper New York State, by Vidich and Bensman. Not only was this community recognised by some readers but a few of the individuals described were also identifiable (notably those playing leading roles in the community).[7] Another example that raises the same issue in a slightly different form is Ditton's study of 'fiddling and pilferage' among bread salesmen. He opens the preface to his book in the following way:

I am lucky enough to have a number of friends and colleagues. Probably not as many of the former, and perhaps more of the latter now that this book has been published. I don't expect that many of the men at Wellbread's will look too kindly on the cut in real wages that this work may mean to them, and my bakery self would agree with them.

(Ditton 1977:vii)

Consequences for future research

Here it is emphasised that social researchers, and especially ethnographers, rely on being given access to settings by gatekeepers and others involved. Research that is found objectionable by the people studied and/or by gatekeepers may have the result that these people refuse future access to researchers. If this were to happen on a large scale, social science would become virtually impossible. This was one of the main arguments used by Fred Davis in his criticism of Lofland and Lejeune's 1960 covert study of a branch of Alcoholics Anonymous (Davis 1961, Lofland 1961); and by Erikson (1967) against the covert study of an apocalyptic religious group in *When Prophecy Fails* (Festinger *et al.* 1956).

Judging the ethics of ethnographic research

All of the above considerations are important ones, though I am inclined to think that the third is the one that should be given most weight. As with all values, the application of any one of them to a situation must be tempered by consideration of others, including the contribution the research findings make to our knowledge. Howard Becker claims that: 'a good study of a community or organization must reflect the irreconcilable conflict between the interests of science and the interests of those studied, and thereby provoke a hostile reaction' (Becker 1964:276). While this may be an exaggeration, it points to the fallacy of any easy assumption that the researcher and the people studied will see the research in the same way. There will always be considerable potential for conflicting interpretations and interests, and there are no simple, general solutions to such conflicts. The ethical aspects of research, like others, must be viewed from a practical point of view. Take the value of honesty. It is certainly important, but that does not imply that we should always tell the whole truth, or even that we should never lie. We do not do this in everyday life. We are circumspect about whom we tell what, and we may even lie on occasion: not only to preserve our own interests but also sometimes to protect those of others too, even those to whom we are not telling the truth (see Mothersill 1996). In research also what is at issue is not 'to deceive or not to deceive' in abstract, but what and how much to tell whom on what occasion. And much the same applies to the other three values. For example, we must weigh the importance and contribution of the research against the likelihood and seriousness of any harm (to the people involved, to others, or to future access), against the value of being honest, and against any infringement of people's privacy. In the process, we will find conflicting indications, difficult judgements and probably disagreements. Ethical issues are not matters on which consensual decisions can always be made. Readers must try to make the most reasonable judgements they can, in the same way as must the researcher and the people studied, recognising that there can be legitimate differences of view.[8]

In order to illustrate the problems involved in making an assessment of the ethics of ethnographic studies, let me consider briefly the article of mine discussed in Chapter 6, this time looking at it from the point of view of ethics. This study undoubtedly involved deception of the teachers. While I had not specifically told them that I would only be researching classrooms, it seems likely that they would have concluded that this was the case. And I did *not* tell them that I was collecting data in the staffroom; partly because I had not originally intended to do so but later because I feared that this would affect their behaviour, and might even lead them to refuse me continued access to the school. The question of privacy is also relevant since on some definitions what went on in the staffroom might be regarded as private. Certainly it was supposed to be private from the pupils: they were hardly ever allowed to come into that room. Parents and other people from outside the school were also not at liberty to enter the staffroom freely, and even the headmaster seemed to feel himself something of an outsider in this setting. On the other hand, one might argue that the staffroom was a public setting for the teachers in relation to one another, certainly more so than their individual classrooms. And one might also claim that, as public servants, teachers should be open to such scrutiny.

The justification I used to myself at the time for engaging in deception and invasion of privacy was that publication would not have damaging consequences for these teachers, and that the data collected were important and could not have been obtained otherwise. Indeed, I delayed publication to protect the teachers from identification. I have since been criticised for doing this on the grounds that I was, in effect, covering up racism. However, when I tried to publish my analysis of staffroom data in book form, one of the objections raised by the publisher's referees was that it represented a scurrilous attack on the teaching profession.[9] This nicely illustrates the range of different views that will often be found about ethical matters.

My current view of the ethics of this study is that my judgement at the time was basically sound, but that the material should have been published earlier. It was not likely that the school and teachers would have been identified, and so there was little danger of damage being done to their reputations or careers. The publication of the account might possibly have damaged the standing of teachers in general, but this seems very unlikely given that it was presented as a study of a small number of teachers in one school; though the atypicality of that school was only emphasised in the thesis, not in the article. In my view, the deception and invasion of privacy were minimal and were justified, despite the fact that my assessment of the value of the study is now a good deal lower than it was at the time I completed it.

You may or may not agree with my conclusions about the ethics of this piece of ethnography, and by no means all ethnographers would. But the discussion does illustrate something of the way in which factual and value judgements have to be combined and weighed against one another when making an ethical assessment of ethnographic studies, and indeed of other types of research.

Conclusion

This book has been primarily concerned with the task of assessing the value of particular ethnographic accounts from the point of view of their contribution to the research literature. I have outlined an approach to this task in some detail and illustrated its application. In this final chapter I have discussed some other aspects of the process of reading and assessing ethnographic research. I have looked briefly at assessments by practitioners, judgements of the competence of researchers, and discussions of the effectiveness and ethics of particular research techniques. In closing this book I want to reiterate what I said in the Preface about the importance of the reading and assessment of research in the social science community. There is a tendency in ethnographic methodology to emphasise the *doing* of research, either in naive realist terms of discovering reality or in anti-realist terms of the artistry of the ethnographer. In this book I have sought to redress the balance somewhat by emphasising the important role that the reading and assessment of ethnographic research should play. In Chapter 5 I noted that ethnographic studies are not well-coordinated with one another (or with other sorts of research). While reference is made to other research to justify the focus and to support or elaborate the analysis and the conclusions drawn, each study tends to be viewed as a piece of solo virtuosity that must stand on its own. And the preponderant justification given for studies is that they open up new areas to investigation. Much less effort has been put into the checking and extension of previous accounts, and the development and testing of existing theoretical ideas. Perhaps if more attention were given to the assessment of studies this would lead to greater coordination of the efforts of ethnographers, and to more rapid progress in the production of valid and relevant sociological knowledge. That, at least, is the hope on which this book is founded.

Notes

1. My view is rather different to that promoted by those favouring practitioner research. I am not denying that research of some kinds may usefully be carried out by practitioners, nor that this may sometimes produce more valuable results than those generated by specialist research. However, it is no panacea. See Hammersley (1992:ch. 8 and 1993b).

2. For a guide to this literature, see the annotated bibliography in Hammersley and Atkinson (1983). This bibliography is not included in the later (1995) edition of this book, and is now out of date of course. However, some more recent research biographies are discussed in that later edition. There is also a listing of research biographies in the field of education in Walford (1987).

3. See the discussions in Becker (1964), Filstead (1970), Rynkiewich and Spradley (1976), Reynolds (1982, chapters 3 and 4 especially), Burgess (1989) and Homan (1991).

4. See Bulmer (1982b) for a collection of articles discussing the ethics of covert research.

5. Of course, in action research this may not matter. Indeed, the aim may be to see how far behaviour can be changed. See Alison Kelly's discussion of this aspect of the *Girls into Science and Technology* project (Kelly 1985).

6. MacDonald (1974) and Walker (1974). See also Jenkins (1980).

7. Vidich and Bensman (1958). For discussion of the ethical issues, see Vidich and Bensman (1964) and Becker (1964).

8. The idea that there may be irreconcilable conflict between values receives its classic treatment in some of the writings of Max Weber, notably Weber (1958). For a more recent and detailed discussion, see Larmore (1987).

9. Parts have been published in article form. Besides that included in the Appendix, see Hammersley (1981).

Staffroom news

In the past twenty years a considerable body of ethnographic research has been carried out in schools. The bulk of this has focused on classrooms. Such a focus is not unreasonable, of course, since the classroom is the place where one might expect the most important work of the school to take place. But there is much to be learned from looking at other parts of schools, and indeed at other aspects of schooling than teacher–pupil interaction.

One important but neglected area is the structure of social relationships to be found among teachers.[1] This is a key issue in itself from the point of view of the sociology of occupations, but, of course, staff relations are also likely to be a significant factor shaping what occurs in the classroom. This article looks at one aspect of relations among the teaching staff of a small, inner-city, boys' secondary modern school (to which I have given the pseudonym 'Downtown'). It focuses on the exchange of 'news' about pupils in the staffroom and seeks to identify its functions.[2]

In the morning, before school starts, the teachers at Downtown sit or stand around in the staffroom reading papers, chatting and smoking. At dinnertime they eat in the hall with the pupils and then come to the staffroom, or eat sandwiches in the staff-room and stay there until afternoon lessons begin, talking, playing cards, etc. During free periods they read newspapers, chat with whoever happens to be there, or mark books.

While there was some variation in who sat where, there were informal groups centred on each of the three coffee tables in the staffroom. For much of the time the three tables formed self-contained interaction groups, although the staffroom as a whole was occasionally the audience. At other times, smaller standing or sitting groups straddling the usual ones were formed.

The typical distribution of the teachers across the three tables partly reflected friendship networks, but the tables were also sites for different activities. Table 1 was invariably occupied with bridge at lunchtime and sometimes at break. Table 2 was often a solo whist game at lunchtime. A regular member of Table 3 mentioned that at one time they had done crosswords though during the period of fieldwork they merely talked, ate sandwiches and read newspapers.

Talk was undoubtedly the major staffroom activity, ranging in focus from football to classical music. However, most staffroom conversation was shop talk, and usually about Downtown and its pupils.

Types of staffroom news

A consequence of the structure of the teachers' work situation at Downtown is that while the information acquired by one in the course of his work is likely to be different from that acquired by others, it is nevertheless of potential relevance to the whole staff. This arises in particular from the fact that, because classes move around between them, the teachers all face the same pupils at one time or another. A premium is thereby placed on the gathering and trading of 'news' about pupils.

Some of this 'news' is about specific events:

1. (Greaves enters the staffroom and speaks to the whole room)
   Greaves: Don't anybody hit Storey for a bit, lay off Storey for a week or so everyone.
   T: Why?
   Greaves: His mother's just been in.
   T: What happened?
   Greaves: She came up to me an' said 'I'll push yer glasses through yer face'.
   T: What did you say?
   Greaves: I raised myself up to my full height and said: 'Madam, if you have a complaint you must see the headmaster' and I walked down to the office with her muttering behind me. Anyway, the head saw her off. He told me to hit him on the shoulder in the future, where it doesn't mark. I haven't heard of that before.
   Webster: That's what Freddy Carpenter used to do, lay about the shoulder (*laughter*).
   T: Aye, after he'd kicked them in the crutch. (Greaves mentions that the mother had said that someone else had hit him on Monday)
   Baldwin: I think I hit him yesterday.
   Denison: I kicked him out.
   T: I don't think he went up to games.
   Baldwin: Oh well I can't have hit him then, my conscience is clear.
   Denison: Well, I kicked him out (*laughter*). Oh no, not literally, I think he did go up to games.
   Baldwin: Oh don't say that. (At lunchtime Greaves tells the story again, this time mentioning that Storey's mother was accompanied by another woman)

.T: For support I suppose.

T: What did you do to him?

Greaves: Oh I hit him across the face three. times – he reckons he counted five as his head hit the desk.

T: What had he done?

Greaves: Oh you know what Storey's like, he's one of those lads who acts just at the wrong moment, he goes just too far, just tips the balance.

On other occasions there is a pooling of news about the same event from multiple sources, including information gleaned from the pupils themselves:

2. (Staffroom)

There is talk about a fight that had taken place in the hall, a prefect had hit three fourth year pupils and one of the latter had tried to hit the prefect in the face with a piece of slate (there are builders in the school). The prefect put his hand up to prevent this and his hand was cut. There was much talk about why the prefect had hit the pupils, I think the teachers were in a quandary. On the one hand, he was apparently provoked, on the other prefects are not supposed to inflict physical punishment. One teacher says 'The head is very concerned and came into the classroom and gave the fifth form a rollicking without mentioning the prefect by name.' Another points out that they had had trouble with that form (the fifth form) when it had been a third form. Holton asks: 'Who got the best of it?' There's a discussion between Webster and Denison (the latter very concerned about likely repercussions on the prefect). Webster reports that 'There's a rumour among the boys that a fourth year gang are going to get the prefect, forty of them, it's no joke, they could disable a teacher.' Some comments were also made to the effect that the prefects represented the teachers.

Staffroom news is selected and presented in terms of its relevance to common problems and issues. The two extracts just quoted are clear examples of this. Thus in Extract 1 the account of the irate mother is prefaced by a summary of its implications for colleagues: 'Lay off Storey for a while.' Furthermore, this account relates to some major teacher worries: possible interference by parents, and being prosecuted for hitting pupils. The former concern has been well-documented elsewhere (Becker 1951, Sharp and Green 1975, Lortie 1975) and emerges clearly in this example; the latter came out quite explicitly at other times in the staffroom:

3. (Staffroom: Larson to Walker in MH's presence)

Larson: You ought to be official NUT Convenor.

Walker: I'm only in the NUT for one reason. (Larson looks significantly towards MH)

Larson: In case you get prosecuted for hitting someone.
Walker: That's right.

While the news about the fight in Extract 2 does not include any specific guidance for future action, it too is relevant to a prevailing staff concern: the danger of pupil violence towards teachers. If the pupils can hit a prefect, a representative of the teachers, might they now start attacking the teachers themselves? While as far as I could tell this had never happened, the possibility was mentioned several times in the staffroom and seemed to underly much talk about the pupils:

4. Webster: I don't know what'll happen this term, it'll be a matter of containment, it's the last two days I'm worried about.
    Dixon: We'll be issued with guns for the last two days, Thompson submachine guns mounted on our desks.

5. (Talk about Wilson, a pupil, between Baldwin and MH after a lesson)
    Baldwin: When you face him his chin's up here (about nose level) and I'm fairly tall, it's quite alarming in a physical sense. I wouldn't like to control him for another two years.

This concern about the danger of pupil violence perhaps explains the staff's somewhat ambivalent attitude towards the prefect and his actions in Extract 2. On the one hand, as their representative, he should be respected by the pupils, and to ensure this he must be supported in his dealings with them; just as a teacher must be supported by his colleagues, and in particular by the head (Becker 1951). On the other hand, the teachers were clearly concerned that this prefect's possibly illegitimate action might itself actually spark off physical attacks on them.

Much staffroom news though is not about specific events at all. Some, for example, concerns pupil moods:

6. (Staffroom)
    Webster: 4T are playing up today.

7. (Staffroom)
    Greaves: I don't know what's happened but 3T are working this morning.

8. (Staffroom: Webster to Marsden)
    Webster: What mood's (name) in today?

Who's here and who's absent are also reported; though it is only the presence and absence of 'problem' pupils which seems to be newsworthy:

9. T: All the clowns in that form are away at the moment, (name) was being very stupid.

10. T: Donald Channing has been put into detention centre.
    Greaves: Good. Has Hughes been excluded because of window breaking?
    T: No, because of the nurse.
    Greaves: Oh pity, that means he'll come back. Still I suppose we should be thankful for small mercies.

11. (Denison and Webster talking)
    Denison recounts who in a particular class is away to indicate that it won't be too bad taking 3T. Webster tells how he tried to persuade a pupil to bunk off (i.e. to truant).

12. Greaves: O'Brien's been suspended.
    T: Where from?
    T: By the neck I hope.

13. Webster: (Aldwych) is back, horrible child.

Once again this news is closely tied to classroom concerns and is made relevant by the fact that the pupils pass round from one teacher to another for different lessons. Given the assumption that there are certain 'prime-movers', getting such information may enable a teacher to anticipate how a lesson will go and what problems are likely to arise.

The primary concern underlying all this news is with sources of trouble and the most common kind of staffroom news retains this interest while being even further removed from specific events. Here teachers' current characterisations of problem pupils are exchanged:

14. (Philipson and Baldwin talking about 2T)
    Baldwin: There's seven good lads but there's some little buggers: Short, Cook, Mills, Dunn's top of the list. Arnold's vicious, aggressive, resentful...
    Philipson: (*laughing*) Is that all?
    Baldwin: Richardson, I can get along with him, he's just a bit loud that's all.
    Philipson: Gary's not so bad.
    Baldwin: He's easily led that's his trouble, I get no pleasure out of taking 2T, no pleasure at all. I get more pleasure out of teaching third year classes.

15. (Staffroom)
    Webster: (Name), he's an oaf.
    Walker: Well y'know why, he's stupid, can't even read or write.
    Webster: O'Brien's going off his head.
    MH: (*laughs*)

Webster: It's not just an expression, I mean it, he's going off his head, but nobody does anything about it of course.

What we have here is the trading of summary typifications of pupils. Teachers employ typifications of pupils to guide their actions (Rist 1973, Hargreaves *et al.* 1975).[3] 'Knowing what to expect' from different quarters minimises the cues required to come to some conclusion about what is going on, what is about to happen, who is involved, in what role, and what can be done about it. Knowing what 'type' a pupil is is important, otherwise one might be caught unawares. Teachers' reliance on typifications is heightened by the immediacy of the classroom (Jackson 1968, Doyle 1977) and their responsibility for what goes on there. Yet, at the same time, these features of classroom interaction also minimise the evidence available for the construction of typifications. Given this, it is perhaps not surprising that the teachers at Downtown seem to supplement their own observations with information from colleagues.

Teachers' typification of pupils

There is now a considerable literature on teacher typifications (Hargreaves 1977). The impetus for this derived initially from the concept of the self-fulfilling prophecy (Merton 1957), dramatically and controversially demonstrated in the classroom by Rosenthal and Jacobson (1968).[4] Their experimental approach has been followed up by more ethnographic work, notably that of Rist (1970, 1973), Nash (1973) and Sharp and Green (1975). More recently, however, attention has shifted somewhat, away from the consequentiality of teacher typifications for pupil careers, and towards an examination of their structure and process. Thus, for example, Leiter (1974) investigated the processes by which kindergarten children are assigned to different ability groups within the class and to different classes in the first grade. In doing this he focuses on the structure of social interaction in assessment interviews and assignment meetings, and the typifications and criteria involved in the decisions. Similarly, but this time in the field of secondary education, Hargreaves *et al.* (1975) have developed a complex model of the process by which pupils are typed as deviant and how these types underpin teachers' responses to classroom events.

Most research in this area to date has sought to identify the typifications used by the teachers in the classroom or other assessment settings. While the importance of the staffroom as a place where teachers 'compare notes' about pupils has been recognised (Hargreaves 1972:ch. 12, Hargreaves *et al.* 1975:62–5), the nature of such discussions has not been investigated. But the analysis of staffroom typifications has methodological as well as substantive significance. Existing research on typifications has relied almost entirely on interview data, and questions inevitably arise about the relationship between the typifications elicited in that context and those which are actually operative in the class-room. After all if, as is generally accepted, action is always tailored to the situation in which it occurs, this is no less true of interview talk than of action in any other setting. How much, then, do the typifications elicited owe to the interview context itself? There is no basis for claiming that staffroom talk about pupils is any closer to classroom operative typifications than that elicited in interviews; but it does provide us with another source of evidence.

Crucial to the nature of both staffroom typifications and those elicited in interviews is that they are two-stage productions. In the classroom the teachers are constantly monitoring and making sense of pupil behaviour, and the products of this process are sedimented as typificatory knowledge. We can expect that this material is then reworked to one degree or another to produce staffroom typifica-tions. Unfortunately, there is no direct way of identifying the nature of this production process and how it differs from that involved in interviews. One indirect line of attack, however, is to compare the typifications produced in the two types of context. Thus, for example, one can compare the staffroom typifications reported here with those elicited in interviews by Hargreaves *et al.* (1975).

At a superficial level, at least, the *content* of the typifications produced in the two contexts does not seem all that different. They are both structured around what are generally regarded as the two basic classroom concerns of teachers: order and learning (Stebbins 1975:45). Even though in both sets of data general descriptors are used much of the time (e.g. in Extract 14 'good', 'little buggers', 'vicious', 'aggressive', etc.), it is quite clear that the typifications are formulated in terms of how much trouble the pupil is for the teachers: 'I can get along with him', 'I get no pleasure out of taking 2T'. There may, of course, be more subtle differences in the way in which these themes are handled in the two kinds of data; and, indeed, my subsequent analysis of staffroom talk will suggest that this is likely to be the case.

In one respect typifications in the two contexts are strikingly different. Those reported by Hargreaves *et al.* (1975) are extensive and elaborated, those exchanged in the Downtown staffroom highly abbreviated. An explanation for this immediately suggests itself on the basis of the nature of the two contexts. Where interaction between the same participants is recurrent, processes of routinisation and institutionalisation occur, and interaction becomes more economic; much is taken for granted as no longer needing to be spelt out (Berger and Luckmann 1967). On the other hand, in interactions with relative strangers, and especially strangers who occupy a strange and ill-defined role such as that of researcher, much will be spelt out at length, especially when the researcher encourages long, open-ended responses.[5]

Underlying some staffroom news is a standard set of pupil types. Sometimes the pupils are described as unpredictable and dangerous:

16. Webster: Wilson, he's going to kill someone one day, he's got the killer instinct. How he's changed, you can see the mentality breaking up, he's unstable.

    Denison: You should have seen him loping across the road at four o'clock yesterday, like a prehistoric animal.

On other occasions they are simply 'buggers', 'bastards', 'yobbos' or 'louts', showing little respect for authority and often setting out to cause trouble:

17. (Staffroom)

    Greaves: His balls haven't dropped yet and he's the worst bastard I've had to deal with in eighteen years teaching.

Perhaps the key feature of the 'unstable' and the 'lout'[6] is that there is little a teacher can do to change them; he must simply recognise how they are and deal with them accordingly, for example by avoiding confrontations:

18. (Staffroom)

    Denison: You've got to try and avoid confrontations, although they sometimes force confrontations on you. (He later explained how he had spent twenty minutes telling a class off today.) You could spend all your time trying to persuade or force the reluctant to work, if there are some who are willing to work it's better to concentrate on them.

However, there are some pupils who appear to be louts but are actually more manageable: they are simply 'easily led':

19. (Staffroom)

    Philipson: Gary's not so bad.

    Baldwin: He's easily led that's his trouble.

These three types of pupil relate primarily to the concern with classroom order and possible pupil violence towards teachers. They each pose a threat, though the third is the weak link, the one where pressure may work. Other problem pupils pose more of a nuisance than a threat, they are 'immature':

20. (Classroom talk between Denison and MH after a lesson)
    Denison: (Name's) an immature lad, cards stuffed in his pockets.

The 'immature' do not challenge teacher authority in any serious or effective way, nor are they physically dangerous. Their deviance is simply an irritation, and results primarily from intrinsic interest in 'childish' activities that are proscribed by school rules.

However, despite these standard types, the nature of the pupils is not treated as static, and much news concerns changes in the pupils, almost always for the worse:

21. Holton: Has Mills been suspended then?
    Roach: Well he's here this morning.
    Holton: Oh so he's not been suspended, after all the head's great threats. It's funny that lad should have gone that way in the last few months. Nobody had ever heard of him before. I mean he's been here four years, someone must have heard of him, y'know as an odd fellow, but not for creating violence.

22. (Marsden talking about a particular pupil to other teachers in the staffroom)
    Marsden: He's getting worse, he needs taking to the head, that'd do him good.

23. (Staffroom discussion)
    Holton: I'll tell you who's becoming a very silly lad: X (pupil's name).
    Scott: I pointed that out a few weeks ago, he should be put in front of the head, it's a phase.
    Holton: Everything Jerry Roach (student teacher) told him to do he did in the most silly, stupid way.
    Scott: (And yet) he's potentially one of the best lads, potentially way beyond the rest.
    Holton: The intelligence is there but he will constantly do the wrong thing.

24. (Staffroom discussion)
    Webster: I'll tell you who's turning nasty: Gary.
    Walker: Johns you mean, well that's because he's stupid, he can't read or write. He reminds me of something in an African jungle.

There is considerable agreement on a list of the infamous, but the list changes over time, stars rise and fall.[7]

An important feature of staffroom news at Downtown is the predominant concern with the 'behaviour' of pupils; in other words with those features of them relevant to the problem of maintaining 'order' in the classroom. Only a few staffroom comments included in the data relate to the 'ability' of pupils and their response' to teaching:

25. Philipson: O'Brien is in the top set in Maths.
    Baldwin: (to Philipson) Has O'Brien got anything upstairs?
    Philipson: No, neither has (name), he got an E in the test, oh n'then a B I think.
    T: He doesn't even know his three times table.
    T: Most of them don't.
    Denison: Some of them don't even know how many inches in a foot.

26. Webster: (Name), he's so lazy it takes him twenty minutes to pick up the pencil and twenty minutes to put it down. (Name) looks prehistoric, I wonder if he's on drugs.

27. Webster: Gibbs is dead to the world.

In summary, then, while some staffroom news is concerned with specific events or the moods, presences and absences of particular pupils, most of it reports how the teachers are finding particular pupils troublesome in the classroom and what conclusions they have come to about what can be expected from them. What is involved here is a process of collective sense-making and stock-taking.

The rhetorical functions of staffroom news

It must not be assumed, however, that typifications necessarily have a purely referential function. In the Downtown staffroom typifications of pupils are frequently used in a more rhetorical fashion than the idea of 'comparing notes' or 'stock-taking' suggests, being dismissive as much as descriptive:

28. Webster: They're all louts.

29. (Staffroom)
    Baldwin: X (pupil's name) is bright.
    Denison: Potentially, but he's got a quirk.
    Baldwin: They've all got their quirks I suppose.
    Denison: But his quirks are between wider extremes, he's got a nice side and a nasty side. Most of them have just got quirks within the nasty.
    Baldwin: They are nasty.

(See also Extracts 14, 15, 16, 17, 20, 25, 26, and 27)

Both the form and the content of the accounts given in the staffroom seem to be shaped to this rhetorical function. For example, a striking feature of staffroom news about pupils is that it generally concentrates on the nature of particular pupils rather than describing their actions in detail; and even where their actions are reported these are described without reference to the features of the interactional context in which they occurred:

30. Vaughan: Mills went berserk this morning, he's a bit unstable that lad.

31. Vaughan: Mills really blew his top today. He'll be inside soon I know it, he's going that way.

32. Vaughan: Mills is going to end up on a manslaughter charge.

33. Vaughan: The slightest thing can set him (Mills) off, someone's only got to stand on his toe and he's off.

34. (Vaughan talks about Mills now and last year)
     Vaughan: If he can't conform reasonably to society then society'll have to kick him out and treat him as an exceptional case.
     Philipson: He's got a tremendous persecution complex.

According to all these descriptions, this pupil is liable to explode at any time for no reason at all, 'the slightest thing can set him off'! This is reminiscent of some of Dorothy Smith's (1978) data, and her analysis of the selective contextualisation involved in the story 'K is mentally ill' told by Angela, 'one of the girls':

'Nearly every morning K would cry in the car, being upset about little things, and the girls would comfort her.' In this instance, the reasons for K's crying are taken to be those immediate occasions which were directly observable to 'the girls' and which were 'little things', not sufficient to warrant her weeping. Angela does not raise the possibility that there might have been features of K's biography unknown to her and the others which would provide adequate reasons for K's disposition to cry so readily.

Accordingly, also, it is not a problem or ought not to be problem, for the reader/hearer who properly follows the instructions for how the account is to be read, that no explanation, information, etc., from K is introduced at any point in the account. And it is not, or ought not to be, strange that at no point is there any mention of K being asked to explain, inform, etc. In sum, then, the rules, norms, information, observations, etc., presented by the teller of the tale are to be treated by the reader/hearer as the only warranted set.

(Smith 1978:35)

This 'cutting out' of context occurs in staffroom talk at Downtown even where the events concerned have had important consequences and where a teacher is specifically asked 'what happened' by a colleague (see Extract 1 above). In all the examples of staffroom talk I collected,[8] the setting, including the actions of the teacher, is taken for granted as natural and normal and as warranting certain behaviour. For the teachers the occurrence of that behaviour does not require explanation, and indeed it does not normally constitute staffroom news. What is a recurrent topic for comment and discussion in the staffroom is the 'failure' of pupils to conform to those expectations.

The rhetorical function of staffroom news can also be detected in the kinds of explanation implied in the typifications. For the most part these appeal to psychological characteristics of pupils: moods, character and mental disorder. Thus, in the case of Mills quoted above (in Extracts 30–4), there is apparently something about him, or in him, which makes him 'unstable' and results in him being unable to 'conform reasonably'. Moreover, it seems (see Extract 21 above) that this aspect of his nature has 'emerged' relatively recently, and if it continues he will 'end up on a manslaughter charge' and go 'inside'. In the teacher's account Mills' 'condition' has its own dynamic. All of the psychological characteristics attributed to pupils in these teacher typifications, then, are presented as underlying generative features which produce typical behaviour in diverse contexts; indeed, irrespective of the context. Nor is there any attempt to trace the causation of these features, to ask why the pupils have these moods, for example, or why Mills might have a persecution complex. Even the notion of behavioural contagion, a more sociological theory (Sutherland 1956), is psychologised: some pupils are simply 'easily led'.

There has been some discussion in the literature of the 'ideological' role of psychological explanations, notably in individualising failure, explaining it in terms of the characteristics of the individual rather than in terms of the structure of society (Ingleby 1976, Bowles and Gintis 1976).[9] But, even if the form of explanation employed by the teachers at Downtown does indeed fulfil some larger social function, we must still ask why they adopt it. We cannot assume it is simply because they have the interests of the system at heart. While remote causes may well be involved, these must operate through more proximal phenomena and it is these which are my concern here.

In discussing teachers' reactions to badly behaved and below average pupils, Stebbins (1975:64) suggests the following explanation for the common tendency to blame the pupil:

There is something disquieting about these students to their teachers; despite their often exceptional efforts to instil respect for classroom rules and raise levels of achievement, the latter still fail. Teachers can blame only two sources for their lack of success: themselves or others. As in other conventional occupations, they choose the latter alternative and thus contend that there is an important aspect of the students' lives or personalities affecting their behaviour at school which is beyond their (the teachers') ability to manipulate.

This seems a plausible explanation for the nature of the typifications of pupils that Downtown teachers exchange in the staffroom. But we must ask why it is that these teachers are faced with the choice of blaming either themselves or their pupils. After all, they might equally appeal to the conditions in which they are forced to work or to the nature of the society in which they live as the source of their, and their pupils', problems. To understand why they do not do this I think we have to look at the conception of teaching to which Downtown teachers are committed. Theirs is a very traditional approach to pedagogy, according to which teaching is a skill which one either has or does not have:

35. (Staffroom: Walker and Baldwin talking about resources)
    Baldwin: Sarge and I calculated we needed £700.
    Walker: I couldn't spend £200. Whatever the school it's the teacher that's important, it doesn't matter what books and equipment there are if the teacher's no good.
    Webster: A good teacher can teach in a henhouse.
    Walker: Whatever the school you must teach basically the same material: the basic skills.

In these terms any failure on the part of pupils to 'behave' and 'learn' is the product either of teacher incompetence or of the ignorance, stupidity and/or loutishness of pupils. From this point of view, the characteristics of the pupils referred to in staffroom news represent obstacles to be recognised, not problems that can be solved by the adoption of appropriate methods. In fact, the explanations for pupil behaviour implied in Downtown teachers' typifications of their pupils are not strictly speaking explanations at all, they have the form of predictions and function as excuses (Lyman and Scott 1970). They specify dangers and limits involved in teaching Downtown pupils, rather than being concerned with identifying problems and finding strategies for solving them.

The construction of descriptions of pupils which cut out the context of their behaviour, and the kinds of explanation for pupils' behaviour employed, both operate to explain away poor pupil performances as the product of ineducability. Through trading news in the staffroom about their pupils Downtown teachers defend their collective sense of competence in the face of potentially discrediting evidence.

Conclusion

I have argued that one important function of staffroom news at Downtown is a kind of collective stock-taking in which teachers compare notes and bring themselves up to date about the pupils whom they all face in the classroom. However, this does not provide an entirely satisfactory explanation for the nature of this staffroom news. The form and content of the accounts of pupils which the teachers exchange suggests that these also serve a rhetorical function. They seem to be designed to protect the teachers' professional identities in the face of the threat to their sense of their own competence posed by the behaviour of the pupils. However, it is important to remember that this threat derives in part from the teachers' commitment to 'traditional' teaching. Moreover, the process of collective self-protection which underpins the exchange of staffroom news at Downtown serves at the same time to preserve this commitment from pressure for change.

Notes

1. There has been *some* empirical research in this area. See Lortie (1975), Woods (1979a) and Hitchcock (1983). For valuable, though speculative, discussions see Waller (1967) and Hargreaves (1972 and 1980).
2. Other aspects of staff relations at Downtown are discussed in Hammersley (1980).
3. For the most part these fall into Becker's (1952) categories of relevance to 'teaching' and 'discipline'. Only one example seems to relate to what Becker calls 'moral acceptability':

    Webster: You can smell him two classrooms off.

4. Rosenthal and Jacobson's results have been challenged. See Good and Brophy (1978) for a useful discussion.
5. On this interpretation my evidence is broadly compatible with that of Hargreaves *et al.* (1975). However, this does not necessarily suggest that the findings actually reflect teachers' classroom typifications. It may reflect instead some correspondence at another level between staffroom and interview talk. In fact, elsewhere Hargreaves (1977) actually suggests such a correspondence, dubbing it 'third party talk'. Woods (1979a) also questions the relationship between the kinds of typifications documented by Hargreaves *et al.* (1975) and teachers' classroom practices. In addition, he provides some data which do not fit the superficial contrast I have drawn between staffroom and interview data.

He presents an interview transcript in which the typifications are highly abbreviated. However, there is a possible, and plausible, explanation for this which leaves my argument substantially intact. This is that the distinction between staffroom and interview contexts is analytically unsatisfactory. What is crucial is not the way settings are conventionally defined but how actors actually define them. I suggest that perhaps in Woods' interview the informant treated him as a colleague as much as a researcher, and that this shaped the nature of his response. This fits Woods' account of his research strategy, in Woods (1977) and (1979a). Regarding the more fundamental issue of the relationship between any of these data and the typifications used by teachers in the classroom, at the moment we are simply in the dark.

6. It is of some interest that these two categories of pupil closely parallel some accounts of pupil and youth typifications. Thus 'the mentally unstable' seems to match the 'nutter' among foobtall fans (Marsh *et al.* 1978), the 'louts' are perhaps similar to Willis's 'lads' (Willis 1977).

7. See Hargreaves' (1967) account of the rise and fall of reputations among pupils. I am not suggesting that teachers' perceptions of the rise and fall of pupils as 'louts' will be an accurate representation of reputations among the pupils, though there may be some relation. Note, however, that the two reputations interact (there may of course be more than two). While a pupil's reputation among teachers will be related to his actions, teachers' actions affect pupil reputations and pupil choices of courses of action. While Hargreaves does not mention this, and it goes against his argument in that he seems to see the pupil subculture as autonomous, once established, evidence for this interaction can be found in his account of the beginning of Clint's rise to become 'Cock of the School'.

8. For a discussion of the problems involved in assessing the representativeness of these data, see Hammersley (1984).

9. However, frequently, the falsity of psychological explanations is taken for granted. While I think it can be quite satisfactorily demonstrated that there are social structural conditions for 'success', psychological attributes no doubt also play a role in determining who 'succeeds' and who 'fails'. One should not simply reject a form of explanation on the grounds of unpalatable political implications.

REFERENCES

Abraham, J. (1989) 'Testing Hargreaves' and Lacey's differentiation-polarisation theory in a setted comprehensive', *British Journal of Sociology*, **40**(1):46–81.

Abraham, J. (1995) *Divide and School: Gender and Class Dynamics in Comprehensive Education*, London: Falmer.

Adler, M. and van Doren, C. (1972) *How to Read a Book* (revised edn), Chicago: University of Chicago Press. (First published 1940)

Anderson, R., Hughes, J. and Sharrock, W. (1986) *Philosophy and the Human Sciences*, London: Croom Helm.

Anyon, J. (1981) 'Social class and school knowledge', *Curriculum Inquiry*, **11**(1):3–42.

Arnold, D. (1970) (ed.) *Subcultures*, Berkeley, California: Glendessary Press.

Athens, L. (1984) 'Scientific criteria for evaluating qualitative studies', in N.K. Denzin (ed.) *Studies in Symbolic Interaction*, vol. 5, Greenwich: JAI Press.

Atkinson, M. (1984) *Our Masters' Voices*, London: Methuen.

Atkinson, P. (1975) 'In cold blood: bedside teaching in a medical school', in G. Chanan and S. Delamont (eds) *Frontiers of Classroom Research*, Windsor: National Foundation for Educational Research.

Atkinson, P. (1981a) *The Clinical Experience: The Construction and Reconstruction of Medical Reality*, Farnborough: Gower.

Atkinson, P. (1981b) Personal communication.

Atkinson, P. (1982) 'Writing ethnography', in H.J. Helle (ed.) *Kultur und Institution*, Berlin: Dunker und Humblot.

Atkinson, P. (1990) *The Ethnographic Imagination*, London: Routledge.

Atkinson, P.A. (1992) *Understanding Ethnographic Texts*, Newbury Park, California: Sage.

Atkinson, P., Delamont, S. and Hammersley, M. (1988) 'Qualitative research traditions: a British response', *Review of Educational Research*, **58**(2):231–50.

Atkinson, P., Shone, D. and Rees, T. (1981) 'Labouring to learn? Industrial training for slow learners', in L. Barton and S. Tomlinson (eds) *Special Education: Policy, Practices and Social Issues*, London: Harper and Row.

Ball, S.J. (1981) *Beachside Comprehensive: A Case Study of Schooling*, Cambridge: Cambridge University Press.

Ball, S.J. (1984) 'Beachside reconsidered: reflections on a methodological apprenticeship', in R.G. Burgess (ed.) *The Research Process in Educational Settings*, Lewes: Falmer.

Bateson, G. (1958) *Naven: The Culture of the Iatmul People of New Guinea as Revealed through a Study of the 'Naven' Ceremonial* (2nd edn), Stanford, California: Stanford University Press.

Beattie, G. (1984) *Talk: An Analysis of Speech and Non-verbal Behaviour in Conversation*, Milton Keynes: Open University Press.

Becker, H.S. (1951) 'Role and career problems of the Chicago public school teacher', Ph.D. dissertation, University of Chicago.

Becker, H.S. (1952) 'Social class variations in the teacher–pupil relationship', *Journal of Educational Sociology*, 25(4):451–65.

Becker, H.S. (1964) 'Problems in the publication of field studies', in A. Vidich, J. Bensman and M. Stein (eds) *Reflections on Community Studies*, New York: Wiley.

Becker, H.S. (1966) 'Introduction' to the reprint of C. Shaw (1930) *The Jack Roller*, Chicago: University of Chicago Press.

Becker, H.S. (1970) *Sociological Work*, Chicago: Aldine.

Becker, H.S., Geer, B., Hughes, E.C. and Strauss, A. (1961) *Boys in White*, Chicago: University of Chicago Press.

Becker, H.S., Geer, B., Hughes, E.C. and Strauss, A. (1969) *Making the Grade*, New York: Wiley.

Bell, C. and Newby, H. (1971) *Community Studies*, London: Allen and Unwin.

Berger, P. and Luckman, T. (1967) *The Social Construction of Reality*, London: Allen Lane.

Black, T.R. (1993) *Evaluating Social Science Research*, London: Sage.

Bloor, M. (1978) 'On the analysis of observational data: a discussion of the worth and uses of inductive techniques and respondent validation', *Sociology*, 12(3):545–7.

Blumer, H. (1939) *Critiques of Research in the Social Sciences: An Appraisal of Thomas and Znaniecki's 'The Polish Peasant in Europe and America'*, New York: Social Science Research Council.

Blumer, H. (1969) *Symbolic Interactionism*, Englewood Cliffs, New Jersey: Prentice Hall.

Bowles, S. and Gintis, H. (1976) *Schooling in Capitalist America*, London: Routledge and Kegan Paul.

Brophy, J. and Good, T. (1970) 'Teachers' communications of differential expectations for children's classroom performance: some behavioral data', *Journal of Educational Psychology*, 61(5):365–74.

Brown, R. (1977) *A Poetic for Sociology*, Cambridge: Cambridge University Press.

Bruyn, S. (1966) *The Human Perspective in Sociology: The Methodology of Participant Observation*, Englewood Cliffs, New Jersey: Prentice Hall.

Bryman, A. (1988) *Quality and Quantity in Social Research*, London: Unwin Hyman.

Bulmer, M. (1982b) *Social Research Ethics*, London: Macmillan.

Bulmer, M. (1984) *The Chicago School of Sociology*, Chicago: University of Chicago Press.

Burawoy, M. (1985) *The Politics of Production: Factory Regimes under Capitalism and Socialism*, London: Verso.

Burgess, R.G. (1982) *Field Research: A Sourcebook and Field Manual*, London: Allen and Unwin.

Burgess, R.G. (ed.) (1984) The Research Process in Educational Settings, Lewes: Falmer.

Burgess, R.G. (ed.) (1986) *Key Variables in Social Investigation*, London: Routledge and Kegan Paul.

Burgess, R.G. (1989) *The Ethics of Educational Research*, Lewes: Falmer.

Burney, E. (1979) *J.P., Magistrate, Court and Community*, London: Hutchinson.

Button, G. (ed.) (1991) *Ethnomethodology and the Human Sciences*, Cambridge: Cambridge University Press.

Campbell, D. (1957) 'Factors relevant to the validity of experiments in social settings', *Psychological Bulletin*, **54**(4):297–312.

Campbell, D. and Stanley, J. (1963) 'Experimental and quasi-experimental designs for research on teaching', in N. Gage (ed.) *Handbook of Research on Teaching*, Chicago: Rand McNally.

Carr, W. (1987) 'What is an educational practice?' *Journal of Philosophy of Education*, **21**(2):163–75.

Carr, W. and Kemmis, S. (1986) *Becoming Critical: Education, Knowledge and Action Research*, Lewes: Falmer.

Cherrington, R., Tomlinson, D. and Watt, P. (1987) 'Pinch and Clark's patter merchanting and the crisis of sociology,' *Sociology*, **21**(1):275–80.

Cicourel, A. and Kitsuse, J. (1973) *The Educational Decision-Makers*, Indianapolis: Bobbs-Merrill.

Clifford, J. (1983) 'On ethnographic authority', *Representations*, **1**(2):118–44.

Clifford, J. and Marcus, G. (1986) *Writing Culture: The Poetics and Politics of Ethnography*, Berkeley: University of California Press.

Cohen, A.P. (ed.) (1982) *Belonging: Identity and Social Organisation in British Rural Cultures*, Manchester: Manchester University Press.

Cohen, A.P. (ed.) (1986) *Symbolising Boundaries: Identity and Diversity in British Cultures*, Manchester: Manchester University Press.

Cohen, S. (1980) 'Ethnography without tears', *Urban Life*, **9**(1):25–8.

Cole, J. (1977) 'Anthropology comes part way home', *Annual Review of Anthropology*, **6**:349–78.

Collins, H.M. (1975) 'The seven sexes: a study of the sociology of a phenomenon, or the replication of experiments in physics', *Sociology*, **9**:205–24. Reprinted in B. Barnes and D. Edge (eds) *Science in Context*, Milton Keynes: Open University Press.

Collins, H.M. (1994) 'A strong confirmation of the experimenters' regress', *Studies in the History and Philosophy of Science*, **25**(3):493–503.

Cook, T.D. and Campbell, D. (1979) *Quasi-Experimentation*, Chicago: Rand McNally.

Crapanzano, V. (1980) *Tuhami: Portrait of a Moroccan*, Chicago: University of Chicago Press.

Cressey, D. (1950) 'The criminal violation of financial trust', *American Sociological Review*, **15**:738–43.

Cressey, D. (1953) *Other People's Money*, Glencoe, Illinois: Free Press.

Cressey, P. (1932) *The Taxi Dance Hall*, Chicago: University of Chicago Press.

Dalton, M. (1959) *Men Who Manage*, New York: Wiley.

Danneker, D. and Kasen, J. (1981) 'Anonymous exchanges: CB and the experience of sex typing', *Urban Life*, **10**(3):265–87.

Davis, F. (1961) 'Comment', *Social Problems*, **8**:364–5.

Denzin, N.K. (1978) *The Research Act in Sociology* (2nd edn), New York: McGraw-Hill.

Denzin, N.K. (1997) *Interpretive Ethnography*, Thousand Oaks, California: Sage.

Dews, P. (1987) *Logics of Disintegration*, London: Verso.

Ditton, J. (1977) *Part-time Crime: An Ethnography of Fiddling and Pilferage*, London: Macmillan.

Dobbert, M. (1984) *Ethnographic Research: Theory and Application for Modern Schools and Societies*, New York: Praeger.

Docherty, T. (ed.) (1992) *Postmodernism: A Reader*, New York: Harvester Wheatsheaf.

Douglas, J. (1976) *Investigative Social Research*, Beverly Hills: Sage.

Dorst, J.D. (1989) *The Written Suburb: An Ethnographic Dilemma*, Philadelphia: University of Pennsylvania Press.

Doyle, W. (1977) 'Learning the classroom environment', *Journal of Teacher Education*, **28**(6):51–5.

Duneier, M. (1992) *Slim's Table: Race, Respectability and Masculinity*, Chicago: University of Chicago Press.

Dunning, E., Murphy, P. and Williams, J. (1988) *The Roots of Football Hooliganism*, London: Routledge and Kegan Paul.

Eagleton, T. (1983) *Literary Theory: An Introduction*, Oxford: Blackwell.

Edmondson, R. (1984) *Rhetoric in Sociology*, London: Macmillan.

Emmett, I. (1964) *A North Wales Village: A Social Anthropological Study*, London: Routledge and Kegan Paul.

Engels, F. (1892) *The Condition of the Working Class in England*, London: Allen and Unwin.

Erikson, K. (1967) 'A comment on disguised observation', *Social Problems*, **14**:266–73.

Evans, J. (1983) 'Criteria of validity in social research: exploring the relationship between ethnographic and quantitative approaches', in M. Hammersley (ed.) *The Ethnography of Schooling: Methodological Issues*, Driffield: Nafferton.

Fay, B. (1975) *Social Theory and Political Practice*, London: Allen and Unwin.

Fears, D. (1977) 'Communication in English juvenile courts', *Sociological Review*, **XXV**:1.

Festinger, L., Riecken, H. and Schachter, S. (1956) *When Prophecy Fails*, Minneapolis: University of Minnesota Press.

Fetterman, D. (ed.) (1984) *Ethnography in Educational Evaluation*, Beverly Hills: Sage.

Fetterman, D. and Pitman, M. (eds) (1986) *Educational Evaluation: Ethnography in Theory, Practice and Politics*, Beverly Hills: Sage.

Feyerabend, P. (1975) *Against Method*, London: Verso.

Feyerabend, P. (1978) *Science in a Free Society*, London: Verso.

Fielding, N. (1981) *The National Front*, London: Routledge and Kegan Paul.

Filstead, W. (1970) *Qualitative Methodology*, Chicago: Markham.

Foster, P. (1990) 'Cases not proven: an evaluation of two studies of teacher racism', *British Educational Research Journal*, **16**(4):335–48.

Foster, P. (1996) *Observing Schools: A Methodological Guide*, London: Paul Chapman Publishing.

Foster, P., Gomm, R. and Hammersley, M. (1996) *Constructing Educational Inequality*, London: Falmer.

Frake, C. (1962) 'The ethnographic study of cognitive systems', in T. Gladwin and W. Sturtevant (eds) *Anthropology and Human Behavior*, Washington D.C.: Anthropological Society of Washington.

Frankenberg, R. (1966) *Communities in Britain*, Harmondsworth: Penguin.

Franklin, A. (1994) 'How to avoid the experimenter's regress', *Studies in the History and Philosophy of Science*, **25**(3):463–91.

Freeman, D. (1983) *Margaret Mead and Samoa: The Making and Unmaking of an Anthropological Myth*, Cambridge, Massachusetts: Harvard University Press.

French, J. and French, P. (1984) 'Gender imbalances in the primary classroom', *Educational Research*, **26**(2):127–36.

Furlong, V.J. (1976) 'Interaction sets in the classroom', in M. Stubbs and S. Delamont (eds) *Explorations in Classroom Observation*, Chichester: Wiley.

Gallaher, A. (1964) 'Plainville: the twice studied town', in A. Vidich, J. Bensman and M. Stein (eds) *Reflections on Community Studies*, New York: Wiley.

Galton, M., Simon, B. and Croll, P. (1980) *Inside the Primary Classroom*, London: Routledge and Kegan Paul.

Geertz, C. (1973) *The Interpretation of Cultures*, New York: Basic Books.

Geertz, C. (1988) *Works and Lives: The Anthropologist as Author*, Stanford, California: Stanford University Press.

Gelder, K. and Thornton, S. (eds) (1997) *The Subcultures Reader*, London: Routledge.

Gitlin, A., Siegel, M. and Boru, K. (1989) 'The politics of method: from leftist ethnography to educative research', *Qualitative Studies in Education*, **2**(3):237–53.

Glaser, B. and Strauss, A. (1967) *The Discovery of Grounded Theory*, Chicago: Aldine.

Goetz, J. and LeCompte, M. (1984) *Ethnography and Qualitative Design in Ethnographic Research*, Orlando, Florida: Academic Press.

Good, T.L. and Brophy, J.E. (1978) *Looking in Classrooms*, New York: Harper and Row.

Gordon, M. (1947) 'The concept of subculture and its application', *Social Forces*, **26**:40–2.

Graham, H. (1983) 'Do her answers fit his questions? Women and the survey method', in E. Gamarnikow, D. Morgan, J. Purvis and D. Taylorson (eds) *The Public and the Private*, London: Heinemann.

Habermas, J. (1973) *Theory and Practice*, Boston: Beacon Press. (First published in German, 1963)

Habermas, J. (1987) *Knowledge and Human Interests*, Cambridge: Polity Press. (First published in German, 1968)

Hammersley, M. (1974) 'The organisation of pupil participation', *Sociological Review*, **22**(3):355–68.

Hammersley, M. (1980) 'A peculiar world? Teaching and learning in an inner city school', Unpublished Ph.D. thesis, University of Manchester.

Hammersley, M. (1981) 'Ideology in the staffroom: a critique of false consciousness', in L. Barton and S. Walker (eds) *Schools, Teachers and Teaching*, Lewes: Falmer.

Hammersley, M. (1984) 'The researcher exposed: a natural history', in R.G. Burgess (ed.) *The Research Process in Educational Settings*, Lewes: Falmer.

Hammersley, M. (1985) 'From ethnography to theory'. *Sociology*, **19**(2):244–59.

Hammersley, M. (1987a) 'Some notes on the terms "validity" and "validity"', *British Educational Research Journal*, **13**(1):73–81.

Hammersley, M. (1987b) 'Ethnography and the cumulative development of theory', *British Educational Research Journal*, **13**(3):283–96.

Hammersley, M. (1989) *The Dilemma of Qualitative Method: Herbert Blumer and the Chicago Tradition*, London: Routledge.

Hammersley, M. (1990a) 'A myth of a myth? An assessment of two studies of option choice in secondary schools', *British Journal of Sociology*, **41**(2).

Hammersley, M. (1990b) 'What's wrong with ethnography? The myth of theoretical description', *Sociology*, **24**(4):597–615.

Hammersley, M. (1991) 'A note on Campbell's distinction between internal and external validity', *Quality and Quantity*, **25**:381–7.

Hammersley, M. (1992) *What's Wrong with Ethnography?*, London: Routledge.

Hammersley, M. (1993a) 'The rhetorical turn in ethnography', *Social Science Information*, **32**(1):23–37.

Hammersley, M. (1993b) 'On the teacher as researcher', *Educational Action Research*, **1**(3):425–45.

Hammersley, M. (1995a) *The Politics of Social Research*, London: Sage.

Hammersley, M. (1995b) 'Theory and evidence in qualitative research', *Quality and Quantity*, **29**:55–66.

Hammersley, M. (1997) 'Educational research and teaching, a response to David Hargreaves' TTA lecture', *British Educational Research Journal*, **23**(2):141–61.

Hammersley, M. and Atkinson, P. (1995) *Ethnography: Principles in Practice*, London: Routledge. (1st edn 1983 London: Tavistock)

Hammersley, M. and Turner, G. (1980) 'Conformist pupils?', in P. Woods (ed.) *Pupil Strategies*, London: Croom Helm.

Hannerz, U. (1969) *Soulside: Inquiries into Ghetto Culture and Community*, New York: Columbia University Press.

Harding, W. (1987) (ed.) *Feminism and Methodology*, Bloomington: Indiana University Press.

Hargreaves, D.H. (1967) *Social Relations in a Secondary School*, London: Routledge and Kegan Paul.

Hargreaves, D.H. (1972) *Interpersonal Relations and Education*, London: Routledge and Kegan Paul.

Hargreaves, D.H. (1977) 'The process of typification in the classroom', *British Journal of Educational Psychology*, 47:27–84.

Hargreaves, D.H. (1978) 'Whatever happened to Symbolic Interactionism?', in L. Barton and R. Meighan (eds) *Sociological Interpretations of Schooling and Classrooms*, Driffield: Nafferton.

Hargreaves, D.H. (1980) 'The occupational culture of teachers', in P. Woods (ed.) *Teacher Strategies*, London: Croom Helm.

Hargreaves, D.H. (1996) 'Teaching as a research-based profession: possibilities and prospects', Teacher Training Agency annual lecture, London.

Hargreaves, D.H., Hester, S. and Mellor, F. (1975) *Deviance in Classrooms*, London: Routledge and Kegan Paul.

Harré, R. and Secord, P. (1973) *The Explanation of Social Behaviour*, Oxford: Oxford University Press.

Hart, H., and Honoré, T. (1985) *Causation and the Law* (2nd edn), Oxford: Oxford University Press.

Harvey, L. (1987) *Myths of the Chicago School*, Aldershot, Gower.

Hickrod, L.J.H. and Schmitt, R.L. (1982) 'A naturalistic study of interaction and frame: the pet as a "family member"', *Urban Life*, 11(1):55–78.

Hirst, P.H. (1971) 'What is teaching', *Journal of Curriculum Studies*, 3(1):9–10.

Hitchcock, G. (1983) 'Fieldwork as practical activity', in M. Hammersley (ed.) *The Ethnography of Schooling*, Driffield: Nafferton.

Homan, R. (1978) 'Interpersonal communication in pentecostal meetings', *Sociological Review*, 26:499–518.

Homan, R. (1991) *The Ethics of Social Research*, London: Longman.

Honigmann, J. (1970) 'Fieldwork in two northern Canadian communities' in M. Freilich (ed.) *Marginal Natives: Anthropologists at Work*, New York: Harper and Row.

Ingleby, D. (1976) 'The psychology of child psychology', in R. Dale *et al.* (eds) *Schooling and Capitalism*, London: Routledge and Kegan Paul.

Jackson, P. (1968) *Life in Classrooms*, New York: Holt, Rinehart and Winston.

Jacobson, D. (1991) *Reading Ethnography*, Albany, NY: State University of New York Press.

168   *Reading Ethnographic Research*

Jay, M. (1984) *Marxism and Totality*, Cambridge: Polity.

Jenkins, D. (1980) 'An adversary's account of Safari's ethics of case study', in C. Richards (ed.) *Power and the Curriculum*, Driffield: Nafferton.

Johnson, J.M. (1993) 'Sociological practice', *Symbolic Interaction*, 16(3):291–3.

Kaberry, P. (1957) 'Malinowski's contribution to field-work methods and the writing of ethnography', in R. Firth (ed.) *Man and Culture*, London: Routledge and Kegan Paul.

Katzer, J., Cook, K. and Crouch, W. (1978) *Evaluating Information: A Guide for Users of Social Science Research*, Reading, Massachusetts: Addison-Wesley.

Keat, R. and Urry, J. (1975) *Social Theory as Science*, London: Routledge and Kegan Paul.

Kelly, A. (1985) 'Action research: what is it and what can it do?', in R. Burgess (ed.) *Issues in Educational Research*, Lewes: Falmer.

Kirk, J. and Miller, M. (1986) *Reliability and Validity in Qualitative Research*, Beverly Hills: Sage.

Kolakowski, L. (1978) *Main Currents of Marxism*, vol. III, Oxford: Oxford University Press.

Krieger, S. (1983) *The Mirror Dance, Philadelphia: Temple University Press*.

Kuhn, T. (1970) *The Structure of Scientific Revolutions* (2nd edn), Chicago: University of Chicago Press.

Lacey, C. (1970) *Hightown Grammar*, Manchester: Manchester University Press.

Lacey, C. (1974) 'Destreaming in a "pressured" academic environment', in J. Eggleston (ed.) *Contemporary Research in the Sociology of Education*, London: Metheun.

Larmore, C. (1987) *Patterns of Moral Complexity*, Cambridge: Cambridge University Press.

LeCompte, M. and Goetz, J. (1982) 'Problems of reliability and validity in ethnographic research', *Review of Educational Research*, 52(1):31 60.

Lehman, T. and Young, T. (1974) 'From conflict theory to conflict methodology', *Sociological Inquiry*, 44:15–28.

Leiter, K. (1974) 'Ad hocing in the schools' in A.V. Cicourel *et al.* (eds) *Language Use and School Performance*, New York: Academic Press.

Lejeune, R. (1977) 'The management of a mugging', *Urban Life*, 6:123 48.

Lejeune, R. (1980) 'A note on "The Management of a mugging"', *Urban Life*, 9(1):113–9.

Lessnoff, M. (1974) *The Structure of Social Science*, London: Allen and Unwin.

Lever, J. (1981) 'Multiple methods of data collection', *Urban Life*, 10(2):199–213.

Liazos, A. (1972) 'The poverty of the sociology of deviance: nuts, sluts and perverts', *Social Problems*, 20:103–20.

Lichtheim, G. (1970) *Lukacs*, London: Fontana/Collins.

Light, R.J. and Pillemer, D.B. (1984) *Summing Up: The Science of Reviewing Research*, Cambridge, Massachusetts: Harvard University Press.

Lincoln, Y. and Guba, E. (1985) *Naturalistic Inquiry*, Beverly Hills: Sage.

Lindblom, C. and Cohen, D. (1979) *Usable Knowledge: Social Science and Social Problem Solving*, New Haven: Yale University Press.

Lindesmith, A. (1937) *The Nature of Opiate Addiction*, Chicago: University of Chicago Libraries.

Lindesmith, A. (1968) *Addiction and Opiates*, Chicago: Aldine.

Lofland, J. (1961) 'Reply to Davis', *Social Problems*, **8**:365–7.

Lofland, J. (1966) *Doomsday Cult: A Study of Conversion, Proselytisation and Maintenance of Faith*, Englewood Cliffs, New Jersey: Prentice Hall.

Lofland, J. (1974) 'Styles of reporting qualitative field research', *American Sociologist*, **9**:101–11.

Lofland, J. and Lejeune, R. (1960) 'Initial interaction of newcomers in Alcoholics Anonymous', *Social Problems*, **8**:102–11.

Lortie, D. (1975) *Schoolteacher*, Chicago: University of Chicago Press.

Lundman, R. and McFarlane, P. (1976) 'Conflict methodology: an introduction and preliminary assessment', *Sociological Quarterly*, **17**:503–12.

Lyman, S.M. and Scott, M.B. (1970) *A Sociology of the Absurd*, New York: Appleton Crofts.

Lynch, F.R. (1977) 'Field research and future history: problems posed for ethnographic sociologists by the "Doomsday Cult" making good', *American Sociologist*, **12** April:80–8.

Lynd, R.S. and Lynd, H.M. (1929) *Middletown: A Study in Contemporary American Culture*, New York: Harcourt Brace.

Lynd, R.S. and Lynd, H.M. (1937) *Middletown in Transition: A Study in Cultural Conflicts*, New York: Harcourt Brace.

van Maanen, J. (1988) *Tales of the Field*, Chicago: University of Chicago Press.

van Maanen, J. (ed.) (1995) *Representation in Ethnography*, Thousand Oaks, California: Sage.

McCall, G. and Simmons, J. (1969) *Issues in Participant Observation*, Reading, Massachusetts: Addison-Wesley.

McCarthy, T. (1978) *The Critical Theory of Jurgen Habermas*, London: Hutchinson.

MacDonald, B. (1974) 'Evaluation and the control of education', in B. MacDonald and R. Walker (eds) *Safari: Innovation, Evaluation, Research and the Problem of Control*, Norwich: Centre for Applied Research in Education, University of East Anglia.

McNall, S. and Johnson, J. (1975) 'The new conservatives: ethnomethodologists, phenomenologists and symbolic interactionists', *Insurgent Sociologist*, **V(IV)**:49–65.

Madge, J. (1963) *The Origins of Scientific Sociology*, New York: Free Press.

Marcus, G. and Cushman, D. (1982) 'Ethnographies as texts', *Annual Review of Anthropology*, **11**:25–69.

Marcus, G. and Fischer, M. (1986) *Anthropology as Cultural Critique*, Chicago: University of Chicago Press.

Mars, G. (1974) 'Dock pilferage', in P. Rock and M. McIntosh (eds) *Deviance and Social Control*, London: Tavistock.

Marsh, P., Rosser, E. and Harré, R. (1978) *The Rules of Disorder*, London: Routledge and Kegan Paul.

Marx, K. (1845) 'Theses on Feuerbach', in K. Marx and F. Engels, *Selected Works*, London: Lawrence and Wishart, 1968.

Matza, D. (1964) *Delinquency and Drift*, New York: Wiley.

Matza, D. (1969) *Becoming Deviant*, Englewood Cliffs, New Jersey: Prentice Hall.

Mayhew, H. (1861–2) *London Labour and the London Poor*, London: Cass.

Mayhew, H. (1971) *The Unknown Mayhew*, edited by E.P. Thompson and E. Yeo, London: Merlin Press.

Merton, R.K. (1957) *Social Theory and Social Structure*, New York: Free Press.

Merton, R.K. (1973) *The Sociology of Science*, Chicago: University of Chicago Press.

Mies, M. (1983) 'Towards a methodology for feminist research', in G. Bowles and R. Klein (eds) *Theories of Women's Studies*, London: Routledge.

Mies, M. (1991) 'Women's research or feminist research? The debate surrounding feminist science and methodology', in M.M. Fonow and J.A. Cook (eds) *Beyond Methodology: Feminist Scholarship as Lived Research*, Bloomington: Indiana University Press.

Miles, M. and Huberman (1984) *Qualitative Data Analysis*, Beverly Hills: Sage. (Second edition, 1994)

Mothersill, M. (1996) 'Some questions about truthfulness and lying', *Social Research*, **63**(3):913–29.

Nash, R. (1973) *Classrooms Observed*, London: Routledge and Kegan Paul.

Newton, K.M. (1990) *Interpreting the Text: A Critical Introduction to the Theory and Practice of Literary Interpretation*, New York: Harvester-Wheatsheaf.

Newton-Smith, W.H. (1981) *The Rationality of Science*, London: Routledge and Kegan Paul.

Newton-Smith, W.H. (1990) 'Realism', in R. Colby, G. Cantor, J. Christie and M. Hodge (eds) *Companion to the History of Modern Science*, London: Routledge.

Norris, C. (1982) *Deconstruction: Theory and Practice*, London: Routledge.

Ochs, E. (1979) 'Transcriptions as theory' in E. Ochs (ed.) *Developmental Pragmatics*, New York: Academic Press.

Owens, R. (1982) 'Methodological rigor in naturalistic inquiry', *Educational Administration Quarterly*, **18**(2):1–21.

Parker, H., Casburn, M. and Turnbull, D. (1981) *Receiving Juvenile Justice*, Oxford: Blackwell.

Passmore, J. (1978) *Science and its Critics*, London: Duckworth.

Payne, G., Dingwall, R., Payne, J. and Carter, M. (1981) *Sociology and Social Research*, London: Routledge and Kegan Paul.

Pinch, T. and Clark, C. (1986) 'The hard sell: "patter merchanting" and the strategic (re)producton of economic reasoning in the sales routines of market pitchers', *Sociology*, **20**(2):169–91.

Pinch, T. and Clark, C. (1987) 'On misunderstanding the hard sell', *Sociology*, **21**(2):281–6.

Platt, J. (1971) *Social Research in Bethnal Green: An Evaluation of the Work of the Institute for Community Study*, London: Macmillan.

Polanyi, M. (1968) 'The republic of science' in E. Shils (ed.) *Criteria for Scientific Development*, Cambridge, Massachusetts: MIT Press.

Pollard, A. (1984) 'Coping strategies and the multiplication of differentiation in infant classrooms', *British Educational Research Journal*, **10**(1):33–48.

Pollert, A. (1981) *Girls, Wives, Factory Lives*, London: Macmillan.

Popper, K.R. (1959) *The Logic of Scientific Discovery*, London: Routledge and Kegan Paul.

Posner, J. (1980) 'On sociology chic: notes on a possible direction for symbolic interactionism', *Urban Life*, **9**(1):103–12.

Pratt, M.L. (1986) 'Fieldwork in common places', in J. Clifford and G. Marcus (eds) *Writing Culture: The Poetics and Politics of Ethnography*, Berkeley: University of California Press.

Punch, M. (1979) *Policing the Inner City: A Study of Amsterdam's Warmoesstraat*, London: Macmillan.

Quine, W.G. (1974) 'Polarised cultures in comprehensive schools', *Research in Education*, **12**:9-25.

Rainwater, L. and Pitman, D. (1967) 'Ethical problems in studying a politically sensitive and deviant community', *Social Problems*, **14**:357–66.

Reynolds, P. (1982) *Ethics and Social Research*, Englewood Cliffs, New Jersey: Prentice Hall.

Richards, I.A. (1943) *How to Read a Page*, London: Routledge and Kegan Paul.

Richardson, L. (1993) 'How come prose? The writing of social problems', in J.A. Holstein and G. Miller (eds) *Reconsidering Social Constructionism*, New York: Aldine de Gruyter.

Rist, R. (1970) 'Student social class and teacher expectations', *Harvard Educational Review*, **40**(3):411–51.

Rist, R. (1973) *The Urban School*, Cambridge, Massachusetts: MIT Press.

Rist, R. (1977) 'On the relations among educational research paradigms: from disdain to detente', *Anthropology and Educational Quarterly*, **VIII**(2):42–9.

Robinson, W. (1951) 'The logical structure of analytic induction', *American Sociological Review*, **16**(6):812–18.

Rorty, R. (1991) *Objectivity, Relativism, and Truth*, Cambridge: Cambridge University Press.

Rose, A. (ed.) (1962) *Human Behavior and Social Processes*, London: Routledge and Kegan Paul.

Rose, D. (1989) *Patterns of American Culture: Ethnography and Estrangement*, Philadelphia: University of Pennsylvania Press.

Rose, G. (1982) *Deciphering Sociological Research*, London: Macmillan.

Rosenthal, R. and Jacobson, L. (1968) *Pygmalion in the Classroom*, New York: Holt, Rinehart and Winston.

Roth, J.H. (1962) 'Comments on secret observation', *Social Problems*, 9:283–4.

Rowe, J.H. (1965) 'The renaissance foundations of anthropology', *American Anthropologist*, 67:1–20.

Roy, D. (1952) 'Quota restriction and goldbricking in a machine shop', *American Journal of Sociology*, 57:427–42.

Roy, D. (1955) 'Efficiency and the fix', *American Journal of Sociology*, 60:255–66.

Rynkiewich, M. and Spradley, J. (eds) (1976) *Ethics and Anthropology: Dilemmas in Fieldwork*, New York: Wiley.

Sagarin, E. (1980) 'Commentary on "Sociology chic"', *Urban Life*, 9(1):12–14.

Scarth, J. (1987) 'Teacher strategies: a review and critique', *British Journal of Sociology of Education*, 8(3):245–62.

Schegloff, E. (1968) 'Sequencing in conversational openings', *American Anthropologist*, 70:1075–95.

Schofield, J.W. (1990) 'Increasing the generalizability of qualitative research', in E.W. Eisner and A. Peshkin (eds) *Qualitative Inquiry in Education: The Continuing Debate*, New York: Teachers College Press.

Schön, D. (1987) *Educating the Reflective Practitioner*, San Francisco: Jossey-Bass.

Schwab, J. (1978) *Science, Curriculum and Liberal Education*, Chicago: University of Chicago Press.

Sharp, R. and Green, A. (1975) *Education and Social Control*, London: Routledge and Kegan Paul.

Sharrock, W. and Anderson, R. (1986) *The Ethnomethodologists*, Chichester: Horwood/London, Tavistock.

Shaw, C. (1930) *The Jack Roller*, Chicago: University of Chicago Press (reprinted 1966 with an introduction by H.S. Becker).

Shostak, M. (1981) *Nisa: The Life and Words of a !Kung Woman*, Cambridge, Massachusetts: Harvard University Press.

Siegel, H. (1987) *Relativism Refuted*, Dordrecht: Reidel.

Smith, D. (1978) '"K is mentally ill": The anatomy of a factual account', *Sociology*, 12(1):23–53.

Smith, J.K. (1984) 'The problem of criteria for judging intepretive inquiry', *Educational Evaluation and Policy Analysis*, 6(4):379–91.

Smith, J.K. (1989) *The Nature of Social and Educational Inquiry*, Norwood, New Jersey: Ablex.

Smith, J.K. (1993) *After the Demise of Empiricism: The Problem of Judging Social and Educational Inquiry*, Norwood, New Jersey: Ablex.

Smith, J.K. and Heshusius, L. (1986) 'Closing down the conversation: the end of the quantitative–qualitative debate among educational inquirers', *Educational Researcher*, 15(1):4–12.

Spender, D. (1982) *Invisible Women*, London: Writers and Readers Publishing Cooperative Society and Chameleon Editorial Group.

Sperber, D. and Wilson, D. (1986) *Relevance: Communication and Cognition*, Oxford: Blackwell.

Spradley, J.P. (1979) *The Ethnographic Interview*, New York: Holt, Rinehart and Winston.

Spivak, G.C. (1994) 'How to read a "culturally different" book', in F. Barker, P. Hulme, and M. Iverson (eds) *Colonial Discourse/ Postcolonial Theory*, Manchester: Manchester University Press.

Stacey, M. (1960) *Tradition and Change: A Study of Banbury*, Oxford: Oxford University Press.

Stacey, M., Batstone, E., Bell, C. and Murcott, A. (1975) *Power, Persistence and Change*, London: Routledge and Kegan Paul.

Stanworth, M. (1981) *Gender and Schooling: A Study of Sexual Divisions in the Classroom*, London: Women's Research and Resources Group.

Stebbins, R. (1975) *Teachers and Meaning*, New York: Brill.

Stebbins, R. (1982) 'Amateur and professional astronomers: a study of their interrelationships', *Urban Life*, **10**(4):433–54.

Stein, M. (1960) *The Eclispse of Community*, Princeton: Princeton University Press.

Stern, P. (1979) *Evaluating Social Science Research*, New York: Oxford University Press.

Stocking, G.W. (1996) *After Tylor: British Social Anthropology 1888–1951*, New York: Athlone.

Strong, P.M. (1979) *The Ceremonial Order of the Clinic: Parents, Doctors and Medical Bureaucracies*, London: Routledge and Kegan Paul.

Strong, P.M. (1988) 'Qualitative sociology in the UK', *Qualitative Sociology*, **11**(1 and 2):13–28.

Sutherland, E. (1956) *The Sutherland Papers* (edited by A. Cohen, A. Lindesmith and K. Schuessler), Bloomington: Indiana University Press.

Taylor, S.J. (1991) 'Leaving the field: research, relationships and responsibilities', in W. Shaffir and R. Stebbins (eds) *Experiencing Fieldwork*, Newbury Park, California: Sage.

Tiles, M. (1988) 'Science and the world', in G. Parkinson (ed.) *An Encyclopedia of Philosophy*, London: Routledge.

Tocqueville, A. (1966) *Democracy in America*, two volumes, New York: Harper and Row. (First published, in French, in 1835 and 1840.)

Tripodi, T., Fellin, P. and Meyer, H. (1969) *The Assessment of Social Research: Guidelines for the Use of Social Research in Social Work and Social Science*, Itasca, Illinois: Peacock.

Tully, J. (ed.) (1988) *Meaning and Context: Quentin Skinner and His Critics*, Cambridge: Polity Press.

Vidich, A.J. and Bensman, J. (1958) *Small Town in a Mass Society*, Princeton: Princeton University Press.

Vidich, A.J. and Bensman, J. (1964) 'The Springdale Case: academic bureaucrats and sensitive townspeople', in A. Vidich, J. Bensman and M. Stein (eds) *Reflections on Community Studies*, New York: Wiley.

Vidich, A.J. and Lyman, S.M. (1995) 'Qualitative methods: their history in sociology and anthropology', in N.K. Denzin and Y.S. Lincoln (eds) *Handbook of Qualitative Research*, Thousand Oaks, California: Sage.

Walford, G. (ed.) (1987) *Doing Sociology of Education*, London: Falmer.

Walker, D. (1980) *The Oxford Companion to Law*, Oxford: Clarendon Press.

Walker, R. (1974) 'The conduct of educational case study: ethics, theory and procedures', in B. MacDonald and R. Walker (eds) *Safari: Innovation, Evaluation, Research and the Problem of Control*, Norwich: Centre for Applied Research in Education, University of East Anglia.

Waller, W. (1967) *The Sociology of Teaching*, New York: Wiley. (First published in 1932)

Warren, C.A.B. (1988) *Gender Issues in Field Research*, Newbury Park, California: Sage.

Wax, M. (1972) 'Tenting with Malinowski', *American Sociological Review*, 37(1):1–13.

Wax, R. (1971) *Doing Fieldwork: Warnings and Advice*, Chicago: University of Chicago Press.

Weber, M. (1958) 'Politics as a vocation', in H. Gerth and C. Wright Mils (eds) *From Max Weber*, London: Routledge.

West, C. and Zimmerman, D. (1987) 'Doing gender', *Gender and Society*, 1:125–51.

West, W.G. (1984) 'Phenomenon and form in interactionist and neo-marxist qualitative educational research', in L. Barton and S. Walker (eds) *Social Crisis and Educational Research*, London: Croom Helm.

Westley, W. (1970) *Violence and the Police*, Cambridge, Massachusetts: MIT Press.

Whyte, W.F. (1993) *Street Corner Society: The Social Structure of an Italian Slum* (4th edn), Chicago: University of Chicago Press.

Williams, W.M. (1956) *The Sociology of an English Village: Gosforth*, London: Routledge and Kegan Paul.

Willis, P. (1977) *Learning to Labour*, Farnborough: Saxon House.

Winch, P. (1964) 'Understanding a primitive society', *American Philosophical Quarterly*, 1:304–24.

Wolcott, H. (1975) 'Criteria for an ethnographic approach to research in schools', *Human Organization*, 34:111–27.

Woods, P. (1977) 'Stages in interpretive research', *Research Intelligence*, 3(1):17–18.

Woods, P. (1979a) *The Divided School*, London: Routledge and Kegan Paul.

Woods, P. (1979b) 'How teachers decide pupils' subject choices', in J. Eggleston (ed.) *Teacher Decision-Making in the Classroom*, London: Routledge and Kegan Paul.

Znaniecki, F. (1934) *The Method of Sociology*, New York: Farrer and Rinehart.

Zorbaugh, H. (1929) *The Gold Coast and the Slum*, Chicago: University of Chicago Press.

INDEX